Illustration by Eva Percy

Going Under the Radar

My Journey to Diagnosis and Battles with Autism and Mental Health

Luke Miller-Ball

Written with assistance from yourmemoir.co.uk
Cover image: Sarah Fewster

CONTENTS

For my mum, family and loved ones. I hope that by reading this you can truly understand. I would like to thank Marnie Summerfield-Smith of Your Memoir for playing a pivotal role in aiding me on this journey, Karen Stanley of Mabel and Stanley publishing for her continuous support and bringing my book into the world and my friends Sarah Fewster and Eva Percy for their illustrations. Furthermore, I want to sound my appreciation to the friends and family I shared this with prior to publication for their feedback and advice in the process of creating this book.

LAST night our internet was disconnected. We are moving in the next few days. So, it was very stressful. I went downstairs for something to eat. My brother Tee-Jay was there. He was in full meltdown mode.

Yet again, wrong place wrong time.

But I did what I always do. Offered help and support. Not only does seeing him in that state, silently screaming in his own head and saying some awful things, make me feel crap but he lashes out at me and mum, although she was asleep this time.

Tee-Jay has always called me a passive aggressive. But last night I had had enough and stormed upstairs. I suppressed, stored, and took in all his negative energy. From then, until now. So, I am so worked up. Everything is making me angry. But I don't shout. I don't get in people's faces. I don't want to argue or have a confrontation. I store it up.

I tell Mum what happened in a WhatsApp message. It's easier. I suppress and leak it like this. I have done it my whole life and bared the brunt of every bad thing that has happened. I am hurting and I feel helpless. But no one knows or sees it from my perspective.

So, I am sitting here, stressing about the move, the recent loss of a loved one and this endless feeling of abandonment, isolation and "when will this stop?".

When Tee-Jay has one of these moments, he says some dark things. I think these things. But my brain stores them up. It's filled with negativity.

I suppress, I don't express.

Only a handful of times have I blown up due to the build-up. The worst is when I feel bad because I can't help.

I asked Dan to go talk to Tee-Jay after I stormed upstairs. I overheard their interaction. Tee-Jay was calm, explaining. I ask myself why everybody treats me differently? Why do I take everything that's thrown at me?

I was in a dark place before, but honestly, I don't want to do anything today. I am fed up. Whenever something happens to Tee-Jay, I get the backlash. I've shared a room with him most of my life. Not only did no one see I had these conditions, but I also had to take the brunt of it when anything upset Tee-Jay's routine.

I wish I wasn't like this.

PROLOGUE

INTRODUCTION

ONE day you will tell your story of how you overcame what you went through, and it will become someone else's survival guide.

As someone who has suffered with his mental health, there are three main reasons I have decided to have a go at writing my life story.

First, a number of those closest to me have, in recent years, suggested that people could potentially be inspired by what I have overcome. Many who suffer like me on a daily basis might take solace knowing they aren't alone if they read my story. I am stepping out of my comfort zone to not only get a better perspective for myself, but also help loved ones gain a better understanding of what I have endured, and continue to endure, each day.

My second reason is a result of what has been a difficult few years for me; I need to find a new hobby. Something to distract me from the deteriorating world around me; something that would challenge me in a way I had never been challenged before. I have never been fond of writing. But over recent years, having faced difficulty communicating, many have said I am better at writing than I am speaking. I assume it's because I have time to think about what I need or want to say before I type it.

Thirdly - and this is more of a personal reason - I want to gain a better understanding of everything that's happened in my life. I want to identify why people have treated me the way they have. Why I behave and deal with situations in the way that I do. Why I've never felt that I fitted in anywhere. This has always been the case. Most importantly though, I want to find out why I can't do the things many people find second nature.

I hope, in a weird way, that this book could start a trend - particularly for people who suffer with a disability or mental illness - and inspire them to find the courage to write their own life stories. It could help them better understand themselves. It could help loved ones to understand. And it could reach out to the wider community to aid others in better understanding their own challenges and help them see they are not alone.

This will hopefully enhance awareness and acceptance around the world.

Autobiographies and memoirs tend to be about celebrities and famous faces. There are in fact some amazing celebrity advocates for mental health and ASD including: Ryan Reynolds, Jared Padelecki, Patrick and Christine McGuiness, Kristen Bell and Selena Gomez, all of whom I hugely admire. Some are dealing with it personally, but some are parents of somebody on the spectrum or suffering with their mental health.

This is similar with television shows such as After Life with thc brilliant Ricky Gervais, who is one of the more genuine, 'tell it as it is' and wholesome celebrities out there. The show focuses predominantly on mental health and how it can hit anyone and just how bad it can get. It is just one example but there are many shows and movies portraying the severity of mental health and why it needs greater support. As we see it, in which three twenty somethings with autism live together is one of several shows in recent times which focuses on autism. I relate to a number of traits associated with all three of them including the enhanced desire for connection, a number of the stimming techniques portrayed and the struggle to integrate with people as well as handling sensory overload. Both these shows attempt to give as true an interpretation of mental health and ASD as possible. As great as this is in increasing awareness and projecting these pivotal and overlooked conditions/disabilities on a large scale, I believe we all have a story to tell. There aren't enough books about ordinary people facing up to extraordinary difficulties every day of their lives. People want to tell their stories, and others want to read them. With more people aware of mental health issues these days, I believe my book could be useful. One of my friends in fact, has opened their heart to me since reading this book and asked for my advice. If I only help a few, great; but if I can make a difference by helping to increase understanding, this will have been a worthy venture.

I have always felt 'left behind', especially in recent years as many people I know married and started families. I know we shouldn't compare ourselves to others but in this age of social media, it is hard not to. I am, of course, delighted for all my friends and family. But being honest, who wants to be with someone who struggles with two essential elements of any relationship? The first is having an active social life. That includes going out, which most people accomplish easily. I have never been to a concert or festival. I over think an invitation to such an event so much that my anxiety takes over and I just can't go. This will be a familiar theme as we dig deeper into my life. Secondly, in my view, is my inability to communicate or provide financially for my family. Work is hard due to my physical and mental issues. As a result, I feel I will never be good enough for anybody.

Leading on from this, I am going to begin this book by taking something I wrote during what was probably the worst time of my life. It was about four years ago. I wanted to get out of my slump and try again. Part of my efforts involved cycling once a week to a mental health centre known as the Brickfield Centre in Epsom, Surrey. I took some courses there, including creative writing. During one session I was asked: 'If you had a box that you wish you could open, what would be in it?'.

We had 10 minutes to write our answers and share it with the rest of the group. Most responses described physical possessions. But I took a more metaphorical approach. I want to share this early on because four years after I wrote it, I am still trying to achieve it:

> **My true potential**
>
> It's always been there yet it still feels so out of reach. I feel my past and respective conditions have shaped me into this person I don't want to be. My conditions, some which say label me, I have had to deal with my whole life. Namely my lack of confidence, communication and general social difficulties which contribute to this daily fight and have all made my true potential a box I can't quite open.
>
> Despite all this, there have been a number of snippets where I unlocked the box i.e. when I graduated after an arduous seven years of higher

> education, worked in Tenerife as a hotel entertainer and head of mini club, and ran a half marathon at Silverstone, among other proud achievements. Every time I put myself out of my comfort zone, although I feel I'm closing in, a part of me will never reach my full potential due to my conditions and general up and down persona. I have made great strides this year and plan on fulfilling my goals, but my anxiety in particular will always be a barrier in getting where I want to be. Finding happiness and stability is a good first step to reaching my potential. I know I'm capable of so much more although currently my potential is still locked in the box.

The teacher then asked a follow up question: "If you were one day able to open the box, how would it make you feel? Furthermore, what would it look like?".

We had another 10 minutes to put our thoughts and feelings to paper. This is what I wrote, and I still am striving to achieve it today:

> If the box was to someday open and my conditions no longer have a hold of me, I would have no fear of being judged and would feel more comfortable, be more talkative and carefree. My confidence and happiness will no doubt improve also. Without my conditions and confidence issues I would be up and out every day, potentially be travelling the world, have a job I'd enjoy, a family of my own and a great

> and supportive social circle. The problems in my head, although not completely, would drift away.
>
> My true potential would be to look and feel good about myself, **not think of every day as a battle and more as an opportunity**; not look to the past but the future. Be generally happy, confident, and successful as well as being consistent in these actions. Having work, family, a social life, freedom to see the world and having something to do each day. To live life without fears and boundaries would unleash my full potential.

For as long as I can remember, I always felt there was something different about me. Although a number of significant moments have shaped me, there was always an underlying reason for all the bad things that have happened so far.

Despite everything, I have always wanted the best for others; always had good intentions; always tried to see the best in everyone. And, as bad as it sounds, I have always put others first - which is probably partly why I can't remember what it is to be happy.

I am an incredibly sensitive individual; I care greatly about everyone in my life. I even wish those who have wronged me a happy and successful life. And because I hate to see people suffering and seeing what this world has become, I struggle even to watch the news.

Another key thing to mention early on is what I call the 'mental block.' This stops or hinders me from doing most things. Not only does it prevent me from speaking or expressing myself, it makes me over analyse every single situation. Even the most basic of interactions, like saying "Hi" to someone, sends my brain into overdrive and anxiety builds to a point where I just can't do it. I have recently been told the term for my enhanced anxiety. I 'catastrophise' everything and always fear the worst before anything has happened. The more I'm surrounded by people, and the more I need to say, the worse it gets. Physically and mentally, I am always on edge. I think so much and speak so little that I have been, and still am, emotionally drained. The harder the task, the more unlikely I'll do it. I hate confrontation of any kind or getting into an argument. And if I'm put in a situation like that, I will either freeze up or try to get away. There are no exceptions in this. I even struggle to communicate with my family. It gets so bad that I can get too anxious to sit down to dinner with them. So I stay up in my room because I'm scared of dealing with social interactions. And the worse thing is, I don't even understand the reasons for it.

It doesn't get any easier when it comes to going to sleep. That's when my brain goes into overdrive. Some nights it can take hours for me to fall asleep. I have always struggled with big crowds, confined spaces and certain bright lights, which make some outings particularly challenging. I hate to let others down, so in the past I have been a bit of a "yes man". More recently, however, I have grown wiser and more willing to say "No" if it is too much for me.

Another term I recently came across through assessments, is something not many neurotypical people are aware of, and truly explains the many breakdowns/meltdowns I have endured in my life. It is known as autistic burnout. It is when an individual is pushing themselves beyond their actual capabilities, both physically and mentally, to fit in a neurotypical world. Essentially, in masking their autism to fit in, one reaches a state of incapacitation, exhaustion, and loss of function.

It is an overwhelming of life stressors and an inability to obtain relief, in which one reaches a point of shutdown. This can last for a long time and can severely affect autistic individuals in every aspect of life. I feel that I've been affected by autistic burnout many times without knowing what it was. Any mention of breakdown/meltdown within this story could potentially coincide with a case of autistic burnout.

A common trait among the ASD community is developing obsessions or intense interests which vary throughout life. Upon self-exploration, I feel it is important to differentiate obsessions and hobbies. I feel the list below are the ones I've had and still have respectively:

- Thomas the Tank Engine

- Reading children's horror books, mainly Shivers and Goosebumps
- Video games
- Chelsea FC
- Friends the TV series
- All things Spanish (culture, food, language etc.)
- Pokémon/football sticker books/Pogs
- Cheesy pop and Eminem
- Football and Tennis (most sports)
- Collecting DVDS
- TV shows and box sets
- DC/Marvel
- Quiz shows
- Wrestling (IMPACT!)

I feel developing these interests are important to those on the spectrum to maintain their balance of routine, give them something to talk about and possibly give them rare opportunities to fit in. Predominantly, it gives them an escape and can help them feel happier in themselves. The level of intensity of interest determines whether it's a hobby or an obsession. For example, I feel Friends the TV series dictated a large part of my young life. I watched it avidly (and still do on occasion). I literally asked every year for them on VHS, both birthdays and Christmases, back when they were 10 pounds for four episodes! It also fuelled another thing those on the spectrum tend to do, which is collecting things. I actually can't, even now, part with my Friend's videos, despite them being useless nowadays, so they are just stuck in my garage gathering dust.

I wrote the above list to try and identify which were which and how they have shaped my life up until now, for good or bad. I feel some are fads, like Pokémon cards or football stickers and were hobbies of the time, but gaming, quiz shows and football in particular, have always been intense interests, and when unable to watch them or I am distracted while undertaking them, I can get flustered/frustrated.

I have seen first-hand how badly someone on the spectrum can react to being distracted or taken away from their respective obsession. Personally, I have had moments when invested in my video game or a football match where it takes priority over everything else. When someone calls me downstairs, alters my plans, or breaks my concentration, although I'm not a shouter, inwardly I can get immensely distressed. I recall putting my head under a pillow and silently screaming to myself but not to the person causing the frustration, and I also breath really heavily, I guess as a way to let them know I'm bothered by the respective circumstances. If someone invites me to an event (on top of the usual anxieties and catastrophising that comes with that) and there is a certain Chelsea match on or a TV series I need to catchup on or I am in an online game (which people are unable to pause) that I'm invested in, it is very likely I will say no to them. I can think of an extreme example of when my brother was unable to use his PC and access his games. Honestly, throughout the years, with inconsistent connections and internet providers, I was always the recipient of my brother's anger and frustrations in many ways, especially as we shared a room for most of our lives. When the internet cut out in the house and he was unable to play a specific game, his routine was broken, and as such had a full-blown meltdown. Screaming at himself, stimming to calm down and saying really negative things.

Generally speaking, intense interests can lead to anti-social behaviour and furthermore decrease the chances of forming or maintaining relationships with others. It can come across as rude by people who don't understand the need for those on the spectrum to have an escape from the world and to keep themselves within safe and familiar territory. A number of those on the spectrum can however channel or direct their respective passions into potential careers, courses or meaningful occupations, further improving their way of life, fitting into society and just giving their lives structure and stability. For example, if someone had an intense interest in animals then they could undertake a veterinary degree and work with animals for a living giving them the perfect way of fitting in and contributing to society. I feel I tried that when choosing to do a sports and exercise sciences degree and tried to become a tennis coach. It may not have worked out but honestly, I felt so upbeat and confident every time I took to the courts. It gave me an escape, a sense of fitting in and general enjoyment.

Having my respective conditions can be such a challenge, and by reading my story I hope people can take inspiration and never give up. I have always felt I have great mental toughness, amazing resilience, and determination to keep defying the odds, as well as an ability to find a way to get the job done.

There will be varied opinions from the release of this book. Some will see this as a form of attention seeking, but that couldn't be further from the truth, especially as I hate being the centre of attention. Some, however, believe me to be very brave in being so open and honest and revealing large parts (at least what I can recall) of my life story. Personally speaking, I initially wrote this for my mum, immediate family, and closest friends to better understand the battles and struggles I have and continue to face. Through sharing with them I concluded that this could really help a lot of people. After much deliberation and thought I decided to release this and am genuinely petrified of the response. My catastrophising in full effect. I just hope that for those with ASD and mental health conditions, it helps show you that you aren't alone.

This is my life so far to the best of my knowledge.

Mum and I at Mount Teide, Tenerife, in 2011.

FAMILY

Before I begin, I want to introduce my family. Outside of family I have predominantly decided to use only initials (or even no names) for people out of respect to them. My family is large and complex, so bear with me.

I start with the person who brought me into the world. As cliché as it sounds, my mum is the best one I could have ever asked for. Through thick and thin she has stuck by, supported, and been there for me. We've been through a lot in 30 years. But Clare Melanie Ball is one of the most giving, empathetic, loving, strong, hard-working individuals I have ever known. She had me at 16 - a challenge in itself. But she also brought up three other children, mostly on her own. My mum is an incredible woman.

After me came my brother Tee-Jay Ball. Diagnosed with autism at 15, he is someone I have always supported; I've always had his back. Incredibly intelligent, with a fighting spirit I feel is reflected in all members of this family, Tee-Jay has come such a long way over the years. He, like me, has yet to reach his full potential. But have no doubt, one day this will happen. We have, for the most of our lives, shared a room, which, as I'm sure many siblings who have had to do the same will agree, has its ups and downs. Although we are two quite different people, I've always spotted similarities in our behaviour and mannerisms.

Next along was my sister, Summer Ball. Now 24, she, like my mum, inspires me every day because of her attitude to life. Truly one of the most hard working and amazing people I am privileged to know. Now a mother herself, giving me a wonderful nephew, she is the embodiment of what I aspire to be. Moving out, having a family of her own, securing a sustainable job, making wonderful friends, and building an active social life, Summer has all the traits I wish I had.

My final sibling (on my mum's side) is my little sister, Isabelle Ball. Still only 15, she is growing into a wonderful young lady. As with all of us, Isabelle has had to deal with several difficulties. One thing I love about her though is that she keeps on smiling and finds a way to overcome any situation. It seems to me that the females in the family tend to do better than the males. They are more outgoing, confident, successful, while the males tend to be homebodies, have mental health issues and unable to reach their true potential.

So, they were easy to write about. But the next bit is hard. It's about my dad, Barry Miller. The only way to begin really, is to mention his premature departure from my life when I was just three years old. Years ago, he told me the reason he left was to travel to Australia, which was a little hard to take. Even harder to take was the fact he moved to Cornwall where he had three other children, the latest of which is having what seems to be a wonderful life. It's the life I envisioned for my mum and dad, and for us.

But had my parents stayed together, of course, I would not have been blessed with my six siblings. My dad, I can see, is a good person. And on the rare occasions we do see each other, or get in touch, we get on well. But those times are too few and far between. It took me a long time to forgive him for leaving. It's only in the past 10 years that I have started using my full name, Luke Miller-Ball, again. But I'm a forgive-and-forget kind of person – mostly. I still love Dad but I'm disappointed with how things turned out.

As much as I love them, I don't know my siblings on Dad's side as much as I would like to. The fact they live in Cornwall doesn't help. Nonetheless, I am proud of them and happy to have them in my life. First, we have Joseph who is transgender, and goes by the name Emily. When I found this out it surprised me, as it would do most people. But I have grown to accept Emily for who she is. I still remember us as kids playing board games, particularly an interactive one called Atmosfear, which had a DVD to go alongside it. Although we don't speak as much, I am proud of the person she has become and I'm very impressed with what she has achieved.

Next up is my little genius of a sister, Daisy. Again, I wish I knew more about her, but all I have are vague memories of us as children and the one time I left my comfort zone to visit them in Cornwall. I love her and all my family so much and am so proud of the lady she is becoming. Finally, my youngest brother, Alfie, who I haven't even had the pleasure to meet yet. Still a toddler, I love seeing photos of him as he grows. I get mixed emotions when I see pictures of him on social media, and the family on holidays, doing things together. I understand that my dad was young when we were born, but part of me wonders why he couldn't give to me the same love and attention he is giving his other children.

I need to mention two more groups: my grandparents and uncles and aunts on both Mum's and Dad's sides. There are more I could mention here, but they are too many; and some will be mentioned later in this book.

First, my nan Linda – who probably knows more about me than I do – and my grandad Colin, along with my uncles, Jamie and Scott, all of whom have helped me in more ways than they will ever know. Frankly speaking, Grandad is the closest thing I ever had to a father figure. For more than 20 years my nan, grandad and uncles have done so much for me, and I'll never forget this. For the first few years of my life, Mum and I lived with them, and years later we were next-door neighbours. They have been an integral part of my life and were there for me when many others were not.

Then there is my nan, grandad, uncles and aunts on dad's side, who, unlike Dad, were always there for me. They were a massive part of my life until we moved to Surrey, and I will never forget all they did for me. Nan Jean, Grandad David, uncles Tony and John, and aunties Sarah, Claire and Nicola, you have all played such a big part in my life and I'm forever grateful.

There are a number of others; we are a very complicated family. It spans many counties. Although I consider all my brothers and sisters full siblings, I am an only child – Clare and Barry's single offspring. Summer and Tee-Jay are Clare's kids with Justin. Isabelle's parents are Clare and Paul. Dad's new family is the same. Dad and Jo are Daisy and Joseph's parents. Dad had Alfie with Sascha.

Left: Me, Isabelle, Summer and Tee-Jay; right: Emily, Dad, me, and Daisy in Cornwall.

Granny Kath and me in Aylesbury; right: Me in Nan's sink!

Left: Mum and I; right: Grandad Colin and I in Roehampton.

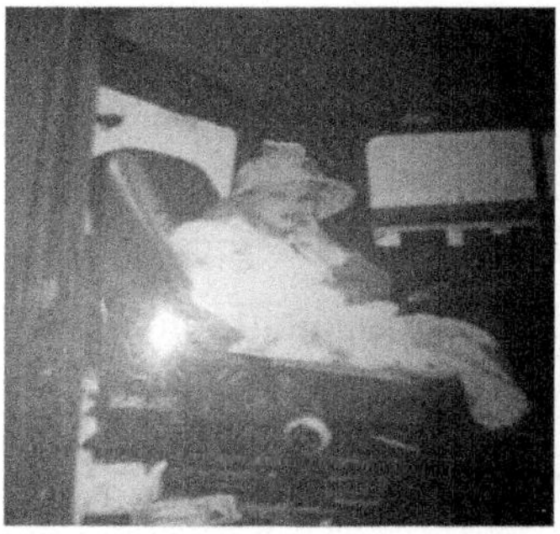

Left: Me at Aylesbury fire station; right: With my aunties, Sarah and Nicola; below: Me in Nan's garden.

Before we get to the main story, I thought it would be nice to share some fun facts:

1. I am technically ¼ Indian (my dad being ½)
2. My first celebrity crush was Amanda Holden (in a show called The Grimleys)
3. My 10 current celebrity crushes are
    - Andrea Londo
    - Jodie Comer
    - Candice Patton
    - Karen Gillan
    - Melissa Benoist
    - Miranda Cosgrove
    - Lily James
    - Adria Arjona
    - Olivia Cooke
    - Summer Bishil
4. My favourite movies are the Back To The Future trilogy
5. My five favourite songs
    - Hall Of Fame — The Script
    - How To Save A Life — The Fray
    - Together Again — Janet Jackson
    - In Too Deep — Sum 41
    - This Is Me — Keala Settle
6. Top 10 TV shows
    - Breaking Bad
    - 24
    - Fringe

- Supernatural
- Sons Of Anarchy
- Boardwalk Empire
- Homeland
- Game of Thrones
- Prison Break
- The Magicians

7. My favourite actors are:
    - Will Smith
    - Jim Carrey
    - Tom Hanks
    - Samuel L Jackson
    - Ryan Reynolds
    - Robert De Niro
    - Robin Williams
    - Arnold Schwarzenegger
    - Adam Sandler
    - Dwayne Johnson
8. It is my ambition to one day be able to work with children in some capacity. I want to help them progress in their education and give them the support I never received. I used to want to be an actor. Even now I'd love to appear in a TV show or movie - DC or Marvel, maybe. Other pipe dreams I had included being an astronaut, fireman, wildlife photographer and footballer. And I'd love to do a voiceover in an animation.

9. I have only been drunk three times in my life. My 18th, 21st and my birthday in Tenerife.
10. I share a birthday with Jim Carrey, James Earl Jones, Michelle Obama, Muhammad Ali, Al Capone and Benjamin Franklin.

COVER SYMBOLISM

- Man - isolated and alone, not knowing where to go or who to turn to, screaming for help but getting no response.
- Sharks - symbols for the ASD and mental health conditions surrounding and consuming the man and closing in with no way of escaping them.
- The island and sea - similar imagery of the loneliness/isolation one feels as they battle each day with these illnesses.
- Plane - representative of society and loved ones. The plane has actively ignored and abandoned the person in need of help and support. The fact it's behind a tree emphasises people hiding away and ignoring the pleas for help.

WHAT AUTISM IS TO ME

AUTISM is known as a spectrum disorder. There are inevitably so many forms and levels of severity to it. People on the spectrum don't tend to like the terms low and high functioning and see us as all under one umbrella. It does however help to show the differences within the spectrum and how every one of us is unique and fighting similar battles every day. One person could be low functioning, unable to speak and in a wheelchair. Another could be high functioning, vocal and able to walk. But there is so much in between. For me, since getting officially diagnosed, my form is a type that goes under the radar, I believe. I may be "high functioning" and, at least on the outside, seemingly a "normal" adult who lives day to day like most other adults do. But this is far from true.

Autism refers to differences with how one's mind works and processes information. But with the form I have, people might just deem you to be shy or the quiet one. When one factors in generalised anxiety disorder and clinical depression among other things, daily life can be exhausting - even when the day consists of doing absolutely nothing. My diagnosis gives me a sense of vindication for all the negative experiences I've faced in life and generally explains so much, particularly when related to my difficulties with communication and social interaction.

Could you envisage a life when you worry about absolutely everything happening around you; where your brain just doesn't stop at any point of the day (distractions such as TV and gaming are rare exceptions); where you fear any encounter with another person; where you are overthinking everything, fearing judgement or ridicule for saying something wrong; where you avoid small talk because you fear it will develop into further conversation in which you - unless sticking to a particular topic or script - are unable to retain information or know what to say in response.

Let me tell you what a day in my life is like. I think of myself being like a battery. How I am depends on the how much I have been charged - how much sleep I have had. I wake up on average at about 40 percent charged.

But as soon as I am up, my brain is already into overdrive. It's the equivalent of opening up ten apps on your phone, some videos too, and music, and leaving them all going so the battery rapidly drains. By lunchtime I'm down to about 25 percent, despite having been slightly re-charged by a shower - though sometimes I can get drowsier after doing that. So, these apps are on all day. And throughout the day, I am working at about a fifth of my capacity. When you add stresses like work, outings and other social stuff, that uses up more of the battery. Sometimes after work, I would pass out after getting home. The worst time is bedtime. My brain is still working. Still thinking about everything. Processing information. But I need to charge the battery (sleep). But my brain doesn't accept this. So, it can take me hours to fall asleep. Throughout the day, my battery levels are at about 20 to 25 percent, which isn't normal or easy; I'm always drowsy and tired.

Over the course of my life, certain people have destroyed my confidence. This has led me to restricting myself with regards to social interaction, going out - things which most people find second nature and take for granted. I have learned to mask certain elements of my condition so well that nobody really thought I was on the spectrum. However, I always knew there was an underlying reason for all I've dealt with and continue to deal with. Accusations have come at me of laziness or being anti-social. Friends and family have alleged that I am missing out on life. Now, though, I have a better understanding of why I am like this. I am overwhelmed by too much information and am naturally a slow processor of data, which accounts for my struggles in general conversation. I never want to hurt anyone or say the wrong thing; I tend to go blank and not know how to respond.

Autism for me is a complex and multi-levelled disorder. No matter the level of functionality, it hampers every individual's day to day life. It can affect them and those around them in so many ways; but for all its negatives, it can also have its positives too. An increased level of honesty, consistency and fairness are examples. I can become intensely interested in a subject or feel great passion for something, and this can be a wonderful thing. For some of us on the spectrum, it can lead to a career in an environment in which they thrive. An ability to persevere and have great attention to detail can also lead to significant achievements.

Since diagnosis, I have noticed several things that I didn't realise I did that are related to autism. For one, when I'm on edge I use several stimming - or self-stimulatory behaviour - techniques to calm myself down or distract myself from whatever causes me to feel uncomfortable. Most think stimming is limited to back-and-forth rocking or hand flapping; but there are so many ways people can stim to calm themselves. I wiggle my toes and bounce my leg quite frequently. I also fiddle with small objects such as a stress ball or anything that's close by, like a toy train, just to distract myself. Mum mentioned that earlier on in life I made coughing noises, as though I was constantly clearing my throat. Rapid eye blinking, staring or "daydreaming", teeth grinding; there are so many other forms of stimming that I've never given a second thought to until recently. If I sing something in my head, as with most things in my life, I have to finish it - it's an OCD thing. However, things like this make sleeping very difficult at times. Like counting sheep or counting down, I have to do this in a specific way to tell my mind it's time to sleep. Some nights this can take hours.

I have always worried about asking for something out of fear of a negative response. Even simple things like, "Can you pass the ketchup?". My anxiety is that bad, that I worry about annoying someone when they are busy doing whatever they are doing. Similarly, when I'm trying to explain something, I overthink to the point that I stress myself out. I say it in a way people will not understand; I only know my way of doing it, so I repeat it, hoping that they will get it the second time round. When they don't, and get frustrated or annoyed, I get upset and disappointed in myself. This is similar with instructions or being asked to do something. I am bad at retaining information, and when I'm put into the spotlight I tend to panic. Most of the time I can complete a task or follow instructions. But when I can't, and there's negative feedback, I take things to heart. I never lash out though and suppress any negative feelings towards that person. Generally, it's because I don't want to annoy or bug someone else. This can happen when I am seeking affection: I am afraid of how the other person will respond; I don't want them to feel uncomfortable. But that fear of being judged or rejected is a horrible feeling. I can be indecisive when put on the spot. I have always been "funny" with big groups or crowds, particularly in a small space such as a bus or a train. I don't like loud noises and bright lights either. At university, I felt so uncomfortable at a disco or club. But I wanted to be with my friends and try to be out my comfort zone. But I have routines and can get flustered if diverted from them.

The biggest challenge - and something most take for granted - is social interaction and communication. Two fundamentals in developing relationships and living a balanced and better lifestyle. It has been the bane of my life being the quiet one and never truly knowing why until now. To be anxious and on edge in literally any interaction with another person, and barely able to ever initiate a conversation, is frightening. To rarely be asked to go to events or hang out with people is devastating. And when I *am* asked, I routinely overthink the situation and work myself up by imagining worst-case scenarios. Eventually, more often than not, I turn the invitation down.

Autism can be debilitating. Being diagnosed at 32 and having to go through childhood and part of my adult life not having any explanation for my negative experiences and daily battles mentally has been arduous. Now equipped with some answers and a greater understanding this will hopefully lead to more support and patience from friends and family. I think what has gotten me this far is that I have always expected a lot of myself. Whenever I failed to meet those expectations, I've tended to break down. I have always wanted to make my family, and particularly my mum, proud. It demoralises me to still be living at home, seeing others achieve what I want to achieve with ease. It genuinely devastates me that I am unable to reach the standards I set myself. But after a lifetime of masking and going through the motions I guess it has taken its toll on me physically and mentally.

After what has been a rollercoaster 30-plus years, with this official diagnosis I can formulate a better way to live with the disorder. With the continued help of loved ones and professionals I can potentially find ways to get the better of my conditions, and eventually get back on track and start to reach my full potential.

I have written my heart out in this book. I hope it helps you understand - it helped me understand all I've been through; all I continue to battle with every day. It has also reaffirmed my belief that I am resilient, mentally strong, and ever willing to keep fighting for those I care about. I hope my story can help people generally understand the diverse nature of Autism and help people with loved ones on the spectrum to remain patient, loving and accepting of them. I see it every day, the differences between myself and my brother - the spectrum is just so wide and varied. We need to start treating everyone on the spectrum equally.

There needs to be more awareness and education about ASD and mental health, and how they can overlap through the course of one's life. How these disorders not only affect the individual in question, but also those around them - and that they may also need additional support. It can be overwhelming for everyone involved and, having shared caring duties with Mum for a long time, I have seen, and continue to see, both sides. It can be an exhausting way of life.

CHAPTER 1

THE EARLY YEARS

BORN on January 17th, 1988 at Queen Mary's Hospital in Roehampton, London, my memories of my first few years are probably the haziest. Through photos, vague recollections, and word of mouth, I can recall certain moments before Tee-Jay was born.

My mum, only 16 when I was born, kept the pregnancy to herself. It wasn't until there was a visible bump that she had to tell loved ones. I was born weighing 4lb 12oz and five weeks prematurely and was kept in a special-care unit for two weeks while I gained weight. Then I was allowed home to meet my family.

Mum returned to school to finish her studies while Nan Linda cared for me. One of my first memories was Mum taking me to Elliott School in Putney - which quite a few of us attended - and introducing me to her friends and one of her favourite teachers. My mum passed me to her teacher, Miss F, who unbelievably dropped me on my head! Skipping forward several years, Miss F ended up teaching me, and always reminded me of that event, embarrassing me in front of my fellow pupils. She was actually a really lovely lady, but that memory always stuck.

For the first few years, my mum and I lived with my grandparents and uncles. Mum would take me out and about: down to visit my other nan, on day trips, to see family members in Aylesbury in Buckinghamshire, and visiting her lifelong friends who would become an extended family. My Nan's house was on Danebury Avenue. It was a two-storey maisonette. The first things that stood out in that house were the pond in the garden, dog Sooty and the large fish tank in the living room. I once walked down the stony garden path and tumbled headfirst onto the pebbled surface. I have the scar to remind me on my forehead.

I have some fond memories of my granddad, and he introduced me to a variety of sports. I used to love the days when we went to play cricket and football in Powell Park. He was an avid Jimi Hendrix fan and I loved to hear him play his guitar. It even got me into music and playing the keyboard. Sadly, my passion faded as the years passed - and to be honest, I was never that good at it. So, it was quite early on that Granddad introduced me to his passions - fishing, music and cricket. We regularly went to the park or to his fishing club in Barnes. I used to love watching him fish, at one with nature, and that's where my love of nature began. He taught me to play cricket, how to bowl and bat and I still love to play. He also taught me to hit a golf ball properly, but I have always been a quite uncoordinated and unorthodox person. There were some incidents, of course. The infamous football episode, for example. I was in goal and Granddad kicked it at me from the halfway line and managed to hit me right on the head. It wasn't one of those soft children's balls, but a proper old-school football. All my family were there for me when I was growing up.

I have memories of outings my mum and other family members took me on - London Zoo, Chessington Zoo, trips to Brighton, regular visits to Aylesbury to see my Great Grandma Kath, uncle, and Aunty Ronnie and Julie, and cousins Lindsey, Matthew and Craig.

There were times we stayed with them, too. My memories, particularly in the early years, are hazy, but I do remember Granny's house vividly. I guess you could say it was my first experience of living in a rural world. Mum and I boarding the train and making our way to Granny's house. The buses coming along once every hour. Shops a 15-minute walk away. Nature and countryside all around us. It was wholly different to living in South-West London.

My grandma lived in a lovely little home and on entering, my first memory is of Gran's little dog, Tammy, and the living room crammed with her memories, photos and ornaments. One recollection that comes to mind is when my Uncle Ronnie took me to an open day at a fire station. We even got to sit in the fire truck; it always stuck in my mind. We spent time at Ronnie's and Julie's house and got to know my cousins, Matthew and Craig. Similarly, we went to visit my cousin Lindsey - I first saw a hedgehog while walking to their house.

My nan and my relatives on my dad's side played an integral role in my upbringing as well. For a large spell, I visited their house at least once a week to see my grandparents, uncles, aunts, and cousins. It was great to be able to see my cousins Jamie and Bradley every week. Every Friday, for many years, we spent hours at my nans watching 90's television, running around the garden (playing a ridiculously repetitive game that incorporated running around in circles saying larger numbers each lap we did), playing football, and later on being glued to the video game Halo. Nan always provided dinner when my granddad, aunts and uncles would come home from work. I can also never forget Nan Jean walking me home and sending me on my way with pocket money, a goody bag of sweets and The Simpsons' comic books. I loved those times and will always treasure them.

Other notable individuals in my early life come in the form of my now extended family, the Morgans, the Busuttils and the Whitbys, among others. In the early years we visited them often and they have, throughout my life, provided my family with love and support, for which I am forever grateful. Paula and the Morgans, who lived on the same road as us, were a big part of my childhood. She lived on the top floor of a flat close to Richmond Park. I used to hate going in that lift; I've never been great with confined spaces. And when we got stuck in the lift, I realised I didn't want to get back in it. So, each time after that that we visited, we had to traipse up and down 11 floors of stairs. I loved going there to see Mark, Nathan and Nicole, and still consider them really close friends. One of my first experiences of anxiety came when I was visiting Nicole. As time passed, it became easier; but I remember struggling severely to speak to her, even from a young age. What stood out from Paula's place was her toilet, oddly. It had the most decorative wall you will ever see, full of flyers and posters from the clubs, gigs and concerts she had attended.

The Whitbys have always been around. Claire is one of my mum's best friends. We have all been on vacations together and had many outings and shared experiences. I remember going to their wedding. I truly do consider them my extended family, and in a weird coincidence, one of Claire's daughters is actually my cousin. I truly adore the family of Claire, Pete, Nikki,

Callum and Samantha. 'Mantha', as she is known, had a crush on me growing up, which I always found funny. I'm proud of the people they have become, and it is always lovely to see them.

The Busuttils again are to me extended family. Carmen is one of mum's best friends, and she has a daughter called Nicole and a son called Beau. They lived in Roehampton before moving to Wandsworth. Sarah, a relative of Carmen's, was my first kiss. I have a nice memory of us outside Carmen's apartment by the window, Sarah kissing me. Lovely girl and now a mother herself. She was a big part of my young life and is forever my friend.

Another early memory was visiting more relatives in Fulham and Kingston. My great grandma, who we called Granny Fulham, we visited semi regularly. I have a vivid memory of their lovely garden. We had to walk down a spiral staircase to access it. I remember walking into my great grandparent's home and being immediately faced with a walk upstairs into what was quite a small and unusual smelling room. We always sat in the living room/kitchen watching TV - a very small black-and-white set. I can't remember for sure, but it may have been one of those old wind-up televisions. We never really went into any other rooms, but my best memories came from helping Granny in the garden, watering the plants and picking berries off the trees.

Even now, this amazing lady never fails to send birthday cards to each of us every year. A truly wonderful person.

My granddad's brother, Steve, and his wife, Tracey, who live in Walton-on-Thames, also received regular visits. They have two children, Caris and Judd, who again were a big part of my childhood. I absolutely adore them all, although as time went by, we slowly drifted apart. Sadly, this is often the case with many familys and friends. But I will always appreciate and care for everyone who has played a part in my life.

One of my earliest memories was watching soap operas with the family. So much so that my first word was actually 'Neighbours'. I recall being bathed as a baby in the sink, listening to Granddad on his guitar and going on outings with Mum and Nan. Regular walks/buggy rides up to Asda on the A3, and on occasion walking through the cemetery on Roehampton Lane. I loved our shopping outings as I got to sit inside the trolley while Mum and Nan did the shopping.

A few months after my father left when I was three, my mum and I moved to Clapham Junction. Around this time, she met Justin Wells and soon became pregnant with Tee-Jay, which led to us having to leave Nan's house due to space issues. After moving to temporary accommodation in a bed-and-breakfast for two weeks, we then settled in a flat on Beauchamp Road. We lived there for about 18 months on one of the cut offs from the main high street. The first thing that always springs to mind when I think of that place is Mr Bean on top of that car riding around after leaving the Arding & Hobbs department store, and also Wimpy around the corner. My only real memory was of Mum buying those miniature cereal multi-packs, which I used to love as you got something different each day. Symptomatic of Mum's hardworking nature, she continued taking me to school in Roehampton. Justin was with us on most evenings and

drove us around in his work van. After a couple of years - I was probably around five or six - we moved to Carslake on the Ashburton estate.

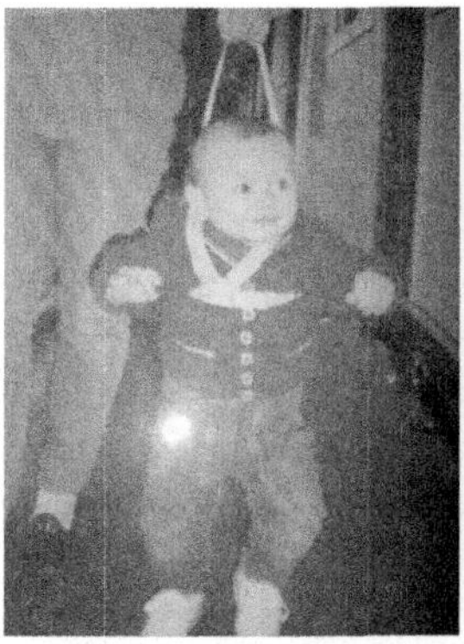

Me on my balcony at Danebury Avenue, and on outings in my early years before Tee-Jay was born.

CHAPTER 2

THE NEW ARRIVAL AND ROEHAMPTON CHURCH SCHOOL

TEE-JAY was born on June 10th, 1992 and was the first of Mum and Justin's two children. My brother's early years were very similar to mine. I didn't feel any different after his arrival. In fact, I was really happy to have a sibling. As the years went by, I found I had more and more in common with him - perhaps due to him playing with similar things, having similar interests to mine, and enjoying similar activities, not to mention that we shared a room for most of our lives.

As a youngster, I had a car mat and a massive interest in toy cars. Tee-Jay and I would line the cars up and argue over who got the 'better' car. We played for hours, driving them around the roads. We also both shared a love of Thomas the Tank Engine. We got the toys, the wallpaper, the bedding and all the videos, which I watched all the time. We were - and still are - both avid gamers too, and one of the first games I remember was a Thomas the Tank Engine puzzle game. But like most siblings, especially in the early days, we had trouble sharing anything and this went on for a few years.

Mum worked at the bakery chain Greggs when we were kids, so we were mainly looked after by our grandmothers. Nan Linda never really took me to baby groups, so there wasn't much interaction with other children until I started at Roehampton Church School when I was four. The only developmental milestone I didn't reach was speech, and recently I was made aware that I had speech therapy around the same time I started school.

Just before Tee-Jay was born, I recall regular visits to Southfields in Wandsworth to Justin's family - who I consider to be my family too - and his mum Yvonne would take care of me. Walking from Putney to Southfields was a trek, although we sometimes took the bus. I remember sitting in Yvonne's living room watching the movies Stand by Me and My Girl, and I can still recall the emotion I got from watching them. Aunty Freddie, I remember, would be in her room watching Formula One. The ornaments, and the memories on the walls, are still vivid. Sometimes we would also visit Aunty Lorraine and our cousins Billy and Danielle. All fond and happy memories.

Of course, some events really stand out. And some I'll never live down. We went to Battersea Park for a family day. We were walking around, and my brother decided to go into a fountain. He didn't realise that the further you went in, the deeper the water got. He couldn't swim at the time and started to struggle. I was frozen to the spot, not knowing what to do. Family members told me to jump in and help. But I just stood there in shock. A stranger, luckily, jumped in and got him to safety. To this day I feel guilty. I should have rescued him. And I think that from that moment on, I took responsibility for Tee-Jay and cared for him. After his experience, he needed an ambulance. He was taken to Charing Cross Hospital. We rode with him. It's the only time I have been in an ambulance. Not only was it a difficult and traumatising experience for me, but Tee-Jay developed a fear of water. Although there were others who could have acted that day, I don't think I ever forgave myself. Recalling experiences like this one will be harder as I continue my story, but I'm going to be open and honest; it's how I've always been.

Fortunately, there are sweeter memories - particularly our outings to Bishops Park. I loved those days. Getting on the bus to Putney; walking over the bridge into the park. A walk by the Thames made me happy; we played on climbing apparatus as we neared the park. The park had a large sandpit as well as the usual swings, slide and climbing frame. My brother and I always enjoyed playing there. So much fun; unforgettable experiences.

I started school in September 1992, and I didn't want to stay. I clung to Mum for dear life and wouldn't go and play with the other kids. I couldn't approach or interact with other pupils and would stay with Mum until the bell went. I hated to deviate or divert or be distracted on the way home from school because I wanted to get back as soon as possible. Mum has always described me as quite precise, and this was evident even in primary school. I always made sure I was prepared for school by packing my bag the night before, and always finished my homework on time. Honestly, I was a goody two-shoes, a perfectionist, wanting to be immaculately dressed; spending time ensuring my collar and tie were correct, and wanting to get changed as soon as I got dirty.

I have always been a follower of rules. I hate making mistakes, upsetting or hurting anyone, and this was the case at school. I believe in treating others how I expect to be treated - and that philosophy has remained intact throughout the roller coaster of the last 30-plus years. I never got detention in primary school; never got told off; always did what I was told. Perhaps this was another early indicator of my anxiety: I didn't want to get in anyone's bad books. I've always believed in being kind, honest and empathetic towards everyone I encounter.

So, my first day at school was terrifying. Fear gripped me as I walked from Nan's house down that now all-too-familiar road, before passing the Shell garage, heading up the hill, before passing the church — and eventually arriving at the gates to reception. There to greet me was the wonderful Miss G, and after much persuasion and holding on to Mum, I was introduced to my classmates. This is where I met SC, now one of my oldest and best friends. But unfortunately, it was also where some of the more negative influences in my life were introduced. They made most of the rest of my school days times I wish I could forget, shall we say. It wasn't apparent from the off because in the early days they were decent. I tried to befriend a few other pupils, and including some of those mentioned, we did form a little group that regularly hung out together. But I only really grew close to SC and KA. Don't get me wrong, I met lots of great people at school - and I'm still in touch with some of them - but it's those two who stand out.

Reception class has vivid memories: watching Spider, an old TV animation; day trips to the common, either to this pan-shaped green area known as the frying pan, or a little further down, the duck pond; lunchtimes having semolina for pudding, or that decorated sponge with custard, under the supervision of the amazing Miss B. Because Roehampton was a Christian school, we attended church under the leadership of Mr M every Wednesday. He reminded me of Jeremy Beadle, the TV practical joker. For the duration of KS1, or Key Stage 1, we stayed in the top half of the school and had breaks in a little playground near the music department. On my last day in reception, I was sad to say goodbye to Miss G. She was so grateful when Mum and I bought her a thank you gift.

Recalling school now, I remember many of the extracurricular activities I enjoyed throughout my time at primary school. Roehampton Library, either reading books - particularly puzzle and multiple-choice storybooks - or using the old 90's computers they had, is a highlight. There, I developed my interest in science and nature through a virtual-reality through-the-body educational game, and I loved playing maze games too. Puzzles I've always loved. Brain training and books like Where's' Wally? I came across them all at the library. Nan also used my library card to take out books, even videos. Sadly, my passion for reading has diminished, but for a large part of my childhood I was obsessed with Nan's books cabinet; fascinated particularly by horror books such as MD Spenser's Shivers series and the

Goosebumps books by RL Stine, as well as these quiz-flip books she had on her shelves.

During summer holidays, half-terms, even after school, I would spend time in the library, but also at Alton Playcentre. It's where I had my first crush. She was called Jessica. Her name is all I remember of her now. But the place itself I recall vividly. The staff were wonderful and gave me my first glimpse into working with children. Sports, arts and crafts, TV and video and even the odd trip to the theatre and the leisure centre, there were so many activities. What kids loved about that place was an area exclusively for well-behaved children. It was known as The White Room within which, as one would guess, the walls were white; but the highlight was a waterbed, which everyone enjoyed. Thinking back, it felt more like a sensory room: lots of lamps, fluorescent lights, different surfaces to touch, calming music, toys, padded walls, mirrors, a ball pit. I used to love it when the staff got competitive. Especially when we played skittles, football or basketball. Such a really nice escape, and something I've never forgotten.

In our busy little lives, we also went to Beavers, Alton Social Club, Putney and Kingston swimming pools and also enjoyed sports including trampolining at Roehampton Club. It was endless and wonderful, but my brother and I were predominantly introvert. We mostly stayed indoors, playing video games, watching children's TV. We've had almost every console over the years and have always been big gamers. TV-wise, I loved CBBC, CITV and Saturday morning TV. Shows that gripped me included The Queen's Nose, The Demon Headmaster, SMTV, ZZap!, Smart, How 2, Thundercats and Tom and Jerry.

Tee-Jay and I loved that Mum worked at Greggs. We got so much free food after school, which was amazing. We also spent a lot of time at Mum's friends' homes. We both loved bike rides too when we were kids. Riding a bike for the first time was quite an adventure. Mum bought me one for Christmas and took me to the common for a test ride. I have always been a bit clumsy, so I don't know why Mum thought it was a good idea for me to have my first go on the bike without stabilisers. But anyway, I hopped on, wobbled forward about two metres, then lost my balance and fell into a large cluster of stinging nettles. Stung from head to toe, I was in absolute agony. Mum rushed me home and bathed me; I was red all over and in so much pain. So, my first memory of cycling wasn't great. But from then on, things improved.

My closest friends during those first few years at school were SC, LA, RV, JO, KA, PL, JM and SR. There were more. But I spent most of my time, in and out of school, with them. We raced over to Richmond Park on our bikes; we climbed trees; we swung on the tyre swing over the creek; we just enjoyed the scenery and the wildlife; we played sports. At one time we even discussed building a robot for the TV series, Robot Wars. Visiting their houses was always fun. We played video games like Mario Kart, Sonic, Streets of Rage, and other games across several consoles but particularly the SNES and Sega Mega Drive.

When I was in Year 1, we moved to Carslake Road on the Ashburton Estate in Roehampton. We got our first pet, a dog, who we named Chelsea. Being a lifelong Chelsea FC fan, it seems quite appropriate that my first pet was named after the club I love. My idol growing up was Frank Lampard and despite Dad trying to make me an Arsenal fan as a toddler, I have always been a true blue. We got him at Battersea Dogs Home, but only had him for a couple of years before we sadly had to give him up. Not all bad though, because he went to live with Selina, a family friend who lived locally, and I still got to see him – until Mum and Selina sadly fell out. It was quite an adjustment for my brother and me to settle into the estate. Neither of us are, nor have been, great with any sort of change. We pushed ourselves to get out, however, and go to the nearby park. It was worthwhile; over the years we made some nice friends including MT, CS, JM, AH, NB, JE, Marcel and Zayn.

My year one teacher was Miss S. In the Christmas pantomime that year, I portrayed one of the Three Wise Men. This panto was a school tradition; I also remember playing an angel and a star.

Outside of school, my mum took me to Kingston. We went to Argos where Mum wanted to buy me a piece of jewellery. It was a ring; I went absolutely crazy and didn't want it. For the longest time, I've had a massive distaste towards any form of jewellery, tattoos, smoking and piercings. But over the years I have become more open minded.

The only things I have ever worn are bracelets and watches. I feel this could be another ASD trait. With rings, for example, I am really iffy when they're on my - or someone else's – pinkie or index finger or thumb. Even when they are on the wedding and middle-finger, I was still quite funny. I feel if I am to ever marry, I will still not be able to have one on my finger; so, I will most likely wear it around my neck.

Smoking is a similar thing. I think it is because a lot of my family over the years have been smokers. I couldn't even touch packs of cigarettes when someone asked me to fetch them. Most people where my Nan lived were smokers, so I was regularly around second-hand smoke, which I hated.

I was seven, maybe eight, and mum was off on a night out. She came to say goodbye. I remember looking at her hooped earrings and absolutely losing it. Mum sent me to my room. I banged on the wall and screamed for ages. Same happened when Mum decided to get her nose pierced, and later in life my sister getting her tongue done. That feeling I get has always been there; I've never understood why.

Tattoos, as I have aged, I've grown more tolerant of. I see them as a form of expression, artistry. And as the cliché goes: Your body is a blank canvas. I also now think each to their own; although when I see a potential partner these things can have a bearing on how I feel about them. Ear cuffs, unusual piercings, and smoking, among other things, do have a detrimental effect on me.

Through life, I have developed attachments to people and things. I can be quite obsessive, I think; but only because I try to love and care for everyone I encounter. Despite never really receiving a lot of it over the years, I have always loved affection and just being good to others. Although with my social and communication issues, alongside my immense anxiety, I over think everything to the point where I rarely act on my thoughts. I also believe this is how people around the world should behave; there is frankly too much hate and misery. I have this habit too where I must touch wood when I have a bad thought about family. I honestly don't know how I will react to another family loss. But superstitiously, I touch wood to make sure they will be okay. Even more odd is every time I walk under any sign, or ladder, I cross my fingers. I have never understood why.

My first obsessions manifested in KS1: football-sticker albums and Pogs (or milk caps as they were also called, a game popular with children in the 1990s). Once I start something, I must try and see it through to the end. This is apparent in almost everything I have done in my life. Learning is a great passion of mine and I spent lots of time as a young child in the library or reading books. My main love was science and nature, and, as I've mentioned, the wonders of the universe. I love Space, the human body and the miracle of our species and galaxy. The way our bodies function is just fascinating, as is the animal kingdom, climates, natural wonders, and the progression of humans and what we have created.

During this time, as a young child, I developed certain routines and repetitive behaviours. One has been ever present. Every time I feel on edge, or need to calm myself down, I put my shirt over my nose and breathe slowly. It's relaxing; I like the material against my face; it calms me down.

Mum says that later in life, I developed an unusual coughing noise, which perhaps could be an anxiety thing or a sign of feeling uncomfortable in a certain situation. I recall something similar with a kind of teeth chattering that used to bug my family. On occasion, similar to the shirt over nose, I rock back and forth to calm myself down; just a few of a number of stimming - or self-stimulatory behaviour - techniques.

Year 2, my final year before heading down the hill towards KS2, was taught by Mrs A. I was still the quiet one; doing similar activities: hanging out with friends, attending the Alton club, spending time in the library and doing activities with the family, including the weekly visit down to my other nan's house.

A bump on the head from this year stays in my mind. It was the year I formed a close bond with KA. Having said that, our friendship didn't begin on the best of terms: she threw me into a bookshelf. But from then on, we grew closer and closer. I remember we even spent one Christmas together - which was when I really fell for her. She stayed over at mine, and we played this strange game that got you sprayed with water. It was a kind of like pinball, with two players. Each time one of us scored, the other got splashed. Our friendship went on until secondary school. She was one of very few girls that I liked, in that way, during primary school. Due to what will become a recurring theme, I suppress so much that anxiety finally takes hold. And more often than not, I cannot take the plunge. Even now, I don't think

KA or some of the other girls I had feelings for were aware I liked them.

It is odd when I look back at school days. I don't remember much from the educational side of things. It's the memories (good and bad) made with friends, and the experiences we shared - in and out of school - that stand out for me. To be fair, there aren't many bad memories from KS1. But that could be me just not remembering, or even blocking out what happened. My earliest negative memories do come from my time in KS2. The beginnings of my love-hate relationship with JO and RV; the drastic change in JM.

To end this chapter positively, let me mention sports days and my abilities as an athlete. I was quite the sprinter over short distances. I recall going up to Dover House Road in Roehampton and taking part in the egg and spoon race, the up-and-under ball race, beanbags into the hoop, skipping, and a host of other events.

These were happier times. I could show what I was capable of without having to communicate; I could just be myself in a race or an event. Receiving adulation from parents, peers and teachers made me feel good; I responded well to this. This was the case throughout school, for example when both my brother and I were in the choir, a play or any production; anything where we could show what we could do. Even Easter competitions such as creating an original Easter hat. I would always try my best to show what I could do.

My mum, Nan and I put a lot of effort into extracurricular activities such as these, both at school and at Roehampton Library. All in all, KS1 was mostly full of positive and uplifting experiences.

Sports day at Roehampton church, above; left: in Nan's garden.

Right, my first day at school; far right: me and one of my obsessions — a computer game

On a day out; and, right, the school's Christmas panto

CHAPTER 3

KS2, CHILD NUMBER 3 AND THE BITE

NOW fully settled at Carslake Road, Mum, on the 2nd September 1995 gave birth to my sister Summer. As with Tee-Jay, the early days with Summer consisted of similar activities we had enjoyed as youngsters. She was my mum and Justin's second child, and we became more involved with Justin's family, seeing them regularly. We often walked up from Putney to Southfields to see Nanny Yvonne and Aunty Freddie. We spent a lot of time playing on a large green at the back of Yvonne's home. We also saw Uncle Steven and our cousin Jordan, Aunty Lorraine and cousins Billy and Danielle, and enjoyed visiting Steven and Tracey and seeing our cousins Caris and Judd, who lived in Walton on Thames.

Not all out visits were fun, however. We went to a family gathering at Uncle John and Aunty Chrissy's home, and their dog bit Summer. She has a small scar on her right cheek now, and for a time, she was scared of dogs.

We obviously continued to enjoy days out at parks and spent a lot of time at our nan's house in Roehampton, and at Mum's friends' homes; there were outings to the beach, shopping trips and visits to theme parks too.

When I was getting ready for Year 3, Tee-Jay was starting school. Now we lived closer to Putney, we had a slightly longer walk to school. It would become a very familiar route for the next decade, until I turned 18. There was the long straight path, crossing over to the common, passing the frying pan and arriving at school.

The enigmatic Miss I taught me in Year 3. A passionate teacher, she demanded the best from her students. One English homework we were set, involved us watching the movie Bugsy Malone. We then had to answer questions based on the film. I struggled; it was the first piece I was unable to complete. I presented a shockingly bad set of answers, which I was ridiculed for. I was absolutely terrified going into school the next day. My anxiety overwhelmed me; I feared I'd let myself and Miss I down.

At home, Tee-Jay and I had adjusted to our new surroundings and made friends on the Ashburton Estate. I had a few school friends such as JE, JM, AH and NB who lived on the estate, and there were some locals we were friendly with too, who we often played with at the park. Around this time, we became friends with the Sandersons, our next-door neighbours. Mother and son respectively, Dawn and Billy have been ever-present in this family for two decades now, and Billy was my brother's first proper friend. Billy soon started spending more time in our home than his own, and practically became a part of the furniture. If you check out some of our family photographs you'll see him photobombing. Other friends included Marcel, MT, CS and Zayn. Tee-Jay was also close pals with CS's younger brother FS because they were in the same year.

We also spent more time with Paula and the Morgans. I was devastated when Paula and family made the decision to move to Hastings. Carmen Busuttil also moved from Roehampton to Wandsworth, so we were travelling around quite a bit. One day we were staying at Paula's house and playing on her bed. I was accidently pushed off and fell on a glass that had been left on the floor. I writhed in pain as blood gushed from my backside. I was taken to the hospital and had to have my right buttock stitched. I've still got the scar.

I have always been a bit clumsy; many people have pointed this out. I also have poor posture, get tired easily and struggle with basic instructions; it's hard to stay focused for long periods of time. Walking home with a friend one day, for example, I was completely oblivious to an oncoming lorry. It came within inches of running me over. Another time, my mum went to collect my brother from school and left me in the car. Clumsily, I let off the hand break. The car started rolling down the hill. My heart was jumping out of my chest. I couldn't move, my whole body was frozen with terror as the vehicle trundled down the road silently. Fortunately, it came to a stop before crashing into anything. That's not my only incident in the car. I was with Justin once, driving along, when for some stupid reason I opened the door and nearly flew out of the moving vehicle. Luckily, Justin reached the door just in time, slamming it shut. Unsurprisingly, I have a phobia about driving. I have terrible spatial awareness and dislike all the responsibility that comes with driving, as well as the costs. Generally speaking, I always made blunders that I feel others wouldn't.

We went to Wandsworth quite a lot. I loved going to the Arndale Centre, which is now known as Southside. Going there with Mum, I enjoyed the pet store, the record shop and Poundland. There was also a little coin ride I recall going on quite a bit, and a toy shop that the kids loved. Visiting the record shop with my mum, I'd listen to an album through headphones. I couldn't help myself sometimes, and once started singing a really cheesy pop song at the top of my voice, I think it was B*Witched. But whatever it was, I was unaware that the entire shop could hear me. The noise-cancelling headphones ensured I was oblivious to what was happening. Mum ran over and stopped me. I was embarrassed, red-faced and ran out of the store.

While we are on the subject of cheesy music, let me admit this now: part of me has always loved a bit of cheese, and I'm not ashamed to say that. I enjoy all sorts of music, but in the 90s this was the type of tune I particularly enjoyed. Nan's probably to blame. She always played cheesy music. But I was a big fan of Steps (Nan's favourites), the Spice Girls, Aqua, Vengaboys, and was massively into S Club 7. I avidly watched their TV show on CBBC. Mum also got me into Abba and the Kisstory radio station. I had a big Britney Spears phase, too, and liked all her older songs.

As well as the music, some of the TV shows my brother and I used to watch included Art Attack, Finders Keepers, The Wild Thornberrys, Jumanji, Hey Arnold!, Recess, and as we went from primary into secondary school, we enjoyed more Cartoon Network, Disney and Nickelodeon shows such as Kenan & Kel, Dexter's Laboratory and Cow and Chicken. I loved those shows. I'm sure it is the same for many of our generation.

As with Wandsworth, I also loved going to Kingston with my family. I loved the old Disney shop they used to have in Bentalls, the department store. You'd walk in and see all the usual toys and such, but this shop was special because at the back they had an Acme Rocket you could go inside. A TV played Looney Tunes cartoons inside the rocket; it was amazing. While mum went shopping, my brother and I sat in the rocket watching cartoons. Mum doesn't remember this, but when I was younger, we attended Christmas light events there and in central London. One year, we saw the Spice Girls turn on the Christmas lights. I loved going to events like that, seeing the effort people put in to brighten up the festive period. Bentalls holds many memories. I believe it is where Tee-Jay and I saw Santa in his grotto (I think we saw him in Clapham too). There was always something going on as you strolled past the escalators towards the balcony: puppet shows, singing teddies and prize-giving events.

Near Bentalls, you find the Kingfisher Leisure Centre. Another favourite spot of mine as a youngster. Often, I was more excited after swimming than by the pool itself. They had a Simpsons arcade game upstairs, you see, and I became obsessed with it. The pool had a wave machine. People swam on one side of the pool for half an hour, waiting for the wave machine to start. Then a surge of waves would start, with people going up and down for about five to 10 minutes, caught up in the wave machine. When I was younger, I spent most of my time in the shallow end with Mum, though. I always had a soft spot for Kingston - going to the market with family members, hearing the butcher in his van selling meat, all the unusual things one can buy at a marketplace, and just genuinely experiencing it all with my family. I even had one of my early birthday parties in McDonald's in Kingston.

Year 4, and we were taught by Miss N. Truth be told, it took me a while to remember her name. That year we had a Greek day. Tons of activities related to Greek food and culture. We even had a sip of wine, I think. As a consequence of that day, I grew to love feta cheese, taramasalata and hummus.

At that time, my feelings for KA were strengthening. But I made the mistake of telling my supposed friend, JM. I feel things started to go downhill at this time, because it was also when I began to be treated badly by a number of classmates. KA was my first major crush, and my feelings lasted several years. I think, to this day, she still may be unaware of how much I cared for her. JM was probably the worst person in primary school. After I told him about KA, he would use it against me - and did so for two years. He blackmailed and manipulated me for a long time; it made for some horrible memories. We were good friends JM and I; I wouldn't have told him otherwise.

We both lived on the Ashburton Estate and walked to and from school together. This provided him with more opportunities to make me feel awful. We also spent a lot of time at each other's houses and went to lots of places such as London Zoo together.

He threatened to expose me to KA, telling her how I felt. This absolutely terrified me. I was a naive child experiencing strong feelings for another for the first time, so each time he threatened to tell her, I freaked out. In turn, it led me to do increasingly demoralising and degrading things for him. To the side of our playground was a hill that led to the common. On that hill, JM humiliated me. We played a game of 'kings and horses'. He was always the king, me the horse. I had to get on all fours and carry him up the hill. If I refused, he'd threaten me with exposure. This went on for ages, and whenever KA was nearby, he would repeat words like 'passion', and say, 'I'm going to tell her.' If this wasn't enough, I was also getting similar treatment from JO and RV. On our bike rides to the common and numerous outings, both in primary and secondary school, they pushed me further and further into a state of depression.

During this time, we had PE in a private swimming pool about 10 minutes down the road. The night before I was due to go swimming, Mum had put my trunks in the wash, and they'd shrunk. Needless to say, I was dreading the next day. Rightly so: it turned out to be another painfully embarrassing experience. We walked down to the centre, got changed and headed to the pool. Unbeknown to me, my trunks were so small that my private parts were sticking out, making it appear as if I had an erection. Of course, the usual suspects noticed this, and I was made to feel awful. Normally not a fan of cold water, I jumped in as soon as possible to avoid further humiliation. They were mocking me, saying I had an erection because I liked a girl called SH, which was not the case.

Honestly, the final few years of primary school were the worst - and things didn't get better as we headed towards secondary school. A familiar theme, as the years went by, was me willing the bell to go during breaks to get out of the playground, away from the social side of my school years. I preferred lessons to free time.

Time away from school tended to be more enjoyable, especially when I visited certain friends' houses, the parks in Roehampton and Putney, and despite being around some people I wasn't too fond of, I loved going to Richmond Park on my bike and climbing trees. I was actually a bit of a daredevil at the time when it came to climbing. At the playground near where we lived, it was almost like we were performing parkour as we raced around the climbing frame and that park. But the inevitable happened, of course. We were all playing, as we usually did, when I thought it would be a good idea to hang upside down on the monkey bars.

I was hanging by my legs, about 12 feet off the ground, when I lost grip and I plummeted, headfirst, to the ground. What made it worse was on the way down I hit my head on a step. I was unconscious for around two minutes, and honestly, when I came to, things were a bit of a blur. Sometimes I wonder how I've survived!

There was joy of course. And what could be more joyous than a first kiss? It was with Sarah. I liked her a lot - as a friend and in the other way too. We spent a lot of time together as kids, so it was no surprise. One day, we went to Wandsworth to visit Aunty Carmen. Sarah and I used to leave the flat and hang out on the landing. We went to the window overlooking Wandsworth. And it happened. Unforgettable in any person's life, this was one of the happier times of my young life.

A couple of years later, we were playing kiss chase in the park where I'd fallen off the monkey bars, and a girl I think liked me was constantly pursuing me during the game. Her name, I believe, was Hannah. She caught up with me, and that was the second girl who kissed me. Aside from the fall off the monkey bars, and something bad that happened later in life, I have a lot of positive memories from that park.

We spent time with a boy called Zayn, who we made friends with, and Tee-Jay and I played Diddy Kong racing and Donkey Kong at Zayn's. Those were happier times. I also went to MT's house, as well as

Marcel's across the road, and those times were also fun. People were mean to Marcel. He had 'an ice-cream head', so called because he had white hair. They even created a theme song for him. Kids can be really cruel. I once went to the swimming pool in Kingston with him, and on the way home we had the roof down in the car, his mum at the wheel, and Janet Jackson's Together Again was playing at full blast. Unfortunately, mine and Marcel's friendship ended on a sour note: he stole money from me. It was a shame; I enjoyed his company.

Back to school and Year five with the wonderful Miss C, who many boys had a crush on. I think this was the first year we had Golden Time. We all looked forward to it on a Friday afternoon. It was 30-60 minutes at the end of the week where we could bring in games and activities from home. I used to love a crazy golf machine game JW brought in. Almost every week I played that with him. During the school week, pupils could lose Golden Time by misbehaving or not doing their work properly. It was a great incentive to always be on your best behaviour.

This was the year I joined the football team. I only remember coming off the bench on occasion, rarely being given the ball and only ever scoring one goal. The usual suspects were in the team, so again I had to deal with them.

We attended a science competition at the local ADT college, which involved lots of schools. We had to build the biggest paper tower, take part in a University-Challenge type quiz, which we came second place in (we were so close to being first), and faced a number of science-related challenges. I remember messing up on one of the pivotal questions: 'What is another name for the electromagnetic spectrum?'. I should've answered 'Rainbow', but I had another moment in which I froze and was unable to answer in time.

My final year in primary school involved a lot of similar incidents. Our final teacher in Roe Church was Mr C; he was a good teacher who wasn't treated well by certain people because of the way he looked without his glasses. Like any exam during my life, the Year 6 SATs caused me great anxiety. I was also dealing with continual bad treatment from classmates due to being a goody two-shoes, and of course the issues surrounding the usual suspects. I was not in a great way heading towards the end of my time at primary school but remained optimistic about secondary school. But after discovering that certain individuals were also attending Elliott (what would be my new school), I feared this was just the beginning. In primary school the one constant who never wronged me was SC. I was, and still am, grateful he is a part of my life. We both had a great passion for

Chelsea FC, and he is one of few who helped me get through school life.

Being in Year 6 had its advantages. We were allowed to sit on the PE benches during assembly while all the rest of the pupils had to be on the floor. Assembly mostly consisted of hymns and announcements for the day. Sometimes awards were handed out. There was a rumour that Tony Adams, the former Arsenal captain, lived across the road from our school. One time we pushed ourselves to knock on his door, but to no avail: probably out training. Each Wednesday we had church. My brother and I were in the choir - Tee-Jay had a wonderful voice. Church was similar to assembly: hymns, sermons and announcements.

Our end of year trip to the Isle of Wight was the first time I left my mum for a sufficient period of time. I remember getting on the coach not wanting to leave her.

After a long journey, including the ferry ride, we got to a place in Cowes called Sandown Bay. We stayed in chalets and undertook a gruelling week of activities, including abseiling down a cliff side, water sports, and rock climbing. That was a wonderful week and a nice end to a rough, few, final years of primary school.

As a little boy, celebrating my sixth birthday.

Getting fit and strong!

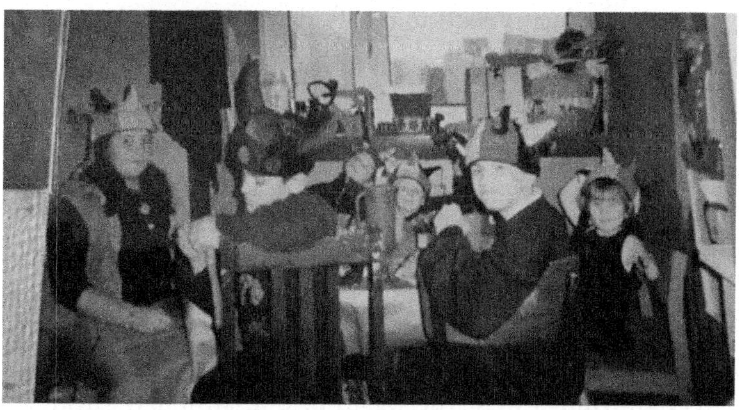

My siblings and me at the Morgans' home with their kids.

CHAPTER 4

THE FOURTH ADDITION, ELLIOTT SCHOOL AND THE DOWNHILL SPIRAL

BEFORE I begin one of the most difficult chapters of my life to date, I want to clarify that this is purely from my perspective. I have only ever wanted the best for others and have never intentionally hurt or upset anyone, although inadvertently this has sometimes been the case. I was a naive and suppressive adolescent who was unable to express or defend himself. I was just trying to fit in, but frankly, with hindsight and the knowledge I now possess, I can see more clearly why certain things went the way they did, although during this awful period I couldn't.

For the people I feel wronged me during this time, I understand you were adolescents too, and to an extent, I have even forgiven some of you. However, the following quote may give you some understanding as to why I had to mention this in the book. I think one of the most humbling lines to live by is, "if someone tells you that you hurt them, you don't get to decide that you didn't". It's not a difficult thing, to take a few steps back and admit that your actions have caused harm to someone you care about.

I feel the following seven years shaped me into the person I am today, alongside the negative experiences earlier in life. It wasn't all bad, but this is the roller-coaster that was Elliott School.

My first day in Year 7, I arrived refreshed and ready to start again - trying to make friends; make the most of my school life. I was placed in 7MH, which refers to the amazing Miss H, who was in charge (this teacher triggered my immense passion for everything Spanish). In a cruel twist of fate, I was placed with two pupils from primary school, one of which I'd had a few issues with. On the plus side I still had SC, but I was also placed in the same tutor group as RV. JO was put into another group, but honestly, for all the bad experiences at Elliott School, I met some lovely people in Year 7. None more so than KH who was frankly my saviour and my favourite person and with whom I spent a lot of time with. This was also the year in which I started wearing glasses. They were round-framed, and the inevitable Harry Potter jokes began.

In the early days, I tried to settle in with my new surroundings integrating myself with friends in my tutor group. Particularly TP, RH, SC, KM, KH, VS and ZS. During the first year, we spent most of our time outside playing games like 'penny up the wall', wrestling and other sports. My Pokémon obsession also began at this time. My brother and I really became addicted to the game, and still have our cards today. When not partaking in some form of activity during break times, I was yet again the quiet one, not knowing why I was like I was. Prior to my diagnosis, it had always been demoralising and debilitating, feeling that I could never fit in; seeing everybody around me doing it with ease. To witness others communicating freely, forming friendships and relationships, going out to events and parties, while I just sat there, the butt of all jokes practically, destroyed me. I felt stifled and like nothing would ever go my way.

Contrary to what many think, I actually only developed feelings for a few people during my seven years at Elliott School. All teens have crushes and attractions, but I only truly fell for around eight or so girls. Over the course of five years, I fell in love with a beautiful Italian girl. IW. Unfortunately, for almost the entire time, she was with other people, including RV and GA, the latter who I believe she is still with to this day. I suppressed it all so much that I don't think she is even aware today of how I felt.

My first crush in secondary school was actually LG. She was sweet and quiet, like myself, and again I don't think she ever knew how I felt. I fell for her during one of our one mile runs in PE. We went up to the common a lot during the years at school and one guy, JC, particularly excelled at sport. A school friend from the time, we went to the Alton club. He was always destined to achieve in the sporting world and is now a professional boxer. He has done incredibly well for himself. So, Year 7 wasn't so bad compared to what was to come.

Before I go on to Year 8, I'd like to stress that it wasn't just me who was going through a rough time. Both my brother and sister were struggling at school. My sister was finding primary school difficult. She had a knife put to her throat on one occasion — primary school kids carrying weapons! This was an early indicator of how bad Roehampton could be and one of the many reasons, over time, why I lost faith in humanity. My mum and Justin also broke up around this time, so we had to deal with that too. Tee-Jay wasn't having it much easier and, like myself, suffered bullying for a large spell of his young life.

Year 8, in fact, was where it all began to get worse; so much worse. My classmates and I spent most of our time indoors during school hours, just sitting and talking. We formed an unofficial lunchtime-table club, I suppose, where we spent most of our break times. These would be some of my worst times. But I had nowhere else to go, so I stuck it out and took everything that was thrown at me. It got so bad that I actually preferred lessons to break times. Not everyone was bad, but as a group they became unbearable. I couldn't defend myself from what they saw as just banter. Although many students got insulted and picked on, I felt I was an easy target because of my inability to communicate or express myself. This continued until sixth form. Individually, there were some good people. BP, for example, became one of my best friends and there was KA, SC and VS. But when in a group, people behave differently; I could never come to grips with that.

A little later, the girls who were our friends took the table next to us and formed their own little group and things got worse. This was at a time when I liked a few of the girls, including one who drastically affected me in the worst way possible. Firstly, I started developing feelings for KH, one of my favourite people. At times, she and her sister RH became like family to me. Unlike with most people, I felt comfortable and at ease with her - a rare plus point. We did everything together, inside and outside of school. For as long as I can remember, I have disliked public transport - confined spaces, loud noises, motion sickness - but I regularly took the bus to Fulham Broadway to see her, and we had some wonderful times. Once, we walked into Putney, sat by the Thames and listened to Maroon 5 CDs. We were so close, and I really miss that.

I also started liking another friend, who I have now known for more than 20 years. I have had on-off feelings for this girl for such a long time, but when I did like her, she was with someone else, so I had to step aside. She is still one of my favourite people and I care about her immensely. As with KH, we spent a lot of time out of school together — in Clapham Junction, Central London and Putney. We walked to Putney together once, visiting her rowing club; she had such a passion for the sport. That was the day I realised how much I liked her. We had some lovely days together, including visiting Waterloo. Despite it being crowded and loud it has always been one of my favourite spots. I love walking along the riverbank and going to the aquarium, arcade and the art gallery. There is also access to Piccadilly circus, the Trocadero entertainment complex and Covent Garden. Out and about in that area, I enjoy listening to buskers, and seeing the Houses of Parliament and the London Eye.

Once at school we visited Canterbury and one of my classmates got lost. Turns out he was looking at antiques and kept us waiting for over an hour. I was also a member of the gifted and talented group, which met in the library to discuss students and announcements we needed to relay to our tutor group. During KS3, I was a member of the athletics team. Although not particularly amazing, I was a 100m sprinter and long jumper. At one of the annual competitions, I was reunited with primary school friends KA and JC. It was lovely to see them again and although the day really dragged on, and our school didn't do particularly well, it was nice to represent Elliott School.

In Year 8 I became a huge fan of the TV show Friends. As with Thomas the Tank Engine when I was younger, I grew so obsessed that every Christmas, one of the few things I asked for was Friends' videos. I watched them avidly and learned a lot. Knowing what I know now, every character experienced some horrible moments. I even tried to mimic Chandler's personality to try and fit in and be like others. If I were to describe myself as three TV characters it would be the personalities (minus the jokes) of Chandler, JD from Scrubs and Mr Bean. In other words, a quiet, unusual, loving, caring, empathetic and sensitive individual. In school, we even formed a Friends fan club; five friends and me. We even took on the names of each of the six main characters. KM is a twin so inevitably became Phoebe, who had a twin, Ursula, on the show. During this time, I also had an Eminem phase, and my brother joined me in this obsession. In what was a hilarious and out-of-character moment, I was sitting in my uncle's room when suddenly Tee-Jay came in dressed as the rapper. He burst into rap, which was obviously recorded by my uncles. He didn't put me off: I'm still a fan!

Around this time, social media and messaging platforms began to become prevalent. I wish I'd never used MSN messenger since it was another way to be picked on, another way to show that I was the quiet one. But it wasn't all bad and led me to become closer with BP and KA in particular. Around this time, we became better friends with our next-door neighbour, Billy Sanderson. We hung out at each other's houses a lot, went to the local parks, on trips, and over time he practically became a part of the furniture. The Sandersons are like extended family to us.

I'd had a difficult day at school and walked home only to realise nobody was at home. I sat on the steps waiting and put my feet up against the window. Without thinking, I started applying pressure to the window, seeing how hard I could push before it broke. I overdid it, smashed it, and felt incredibly awful. Maybe it was me lashing out or maybe it was just a silly moment, but it's something else I can't get out of my head.

That might have been the day of my first detention. Thanks to the entire class behaving stupidly during a lesson we all had to stay after school. Another indicator of my anxiety is when I desperately need the toilet. Arriving home with no one there triggered it because I suddenly needed to go. I just sat there until the last second, in which I decided to knock on Dawn Sanderson's door, but it was too late. I cried my eyes out and was so embarrassed by the whole ordeal. But I remember having that mental block, that fear, and for a time being unable to knock on her door. This has been a recurring theme throughout my life: that mental block I get if I have to communicate with someone.

We were all sitting at the infamous lunchtime table club one dinner time. Everyone was showing off, there was a lot of banter as usual.

Someone said, 'I've never heard you swear before Luke'.

Being a follower of the rules, I didn't really curse until later in life, and I still actively try not to swear in front of too many people.

But the kids picked up on this, and for the entire lunch hour they tried convincing me to swear. No matter what I stuck to my principles and just couldn't do it. Perhaps out of fear of them telling a teacher or my family, or even just simply over thinking the entire situation, I refused.

Then they started crowding around me, taking bets, offering me things if only I swore. It was horrible, and the worst thing was, as in most circumstances, no one defended me. They all knew I was quiet and unable to protect myself and they took advantage of that for such a long time.

Year 8 ended pleasantly. A school trip to Barcelona. The journey was ridiculous though. We went by coach; 27 hours there and back. Suffering motion sickness almost my entire life, that was quite an ordeal. Thankfully, Mum had prepared, and I had travel sickness meds, sweets and a wristband to alleviate my suffering.

The teachers were also aware, so I sat at the front on every trip we went on. There was also a TV on the coach, so the movies were a nice distraction. Despite the travelling, the holiday was lovely. We stayed in a nice hotel and went on a few day trips. We even got to visit Camp Nou, where the legendary Barcelona football team play, that was an incredible experience. We also visited La Sagrada Familia, Gaudi's unfinished basilica, and an amazing theme park called Port Aventura. This was where I got over my fear of rollercoasters by going on a ride called La Stampida. The trip was a delight and enhanced my love of Spain and its culture.

But things would get worse. Year 9 came along, my most difficult time at school. We also moved back to Roehampton; a place called Ibsley Gardens. It was closer to where Nan lived and just up the road from my Aunty Lorraine and Cousin Jamie. It was now a longer walk to school, and another opportunity for the usual suspects (and a few new ones) to make my life hell.

I hated walking to and from school with them, but I had nobody else, and I wanted to stick with the few good ones. Again, as a group, they became unbearable at times. Things continued to spiral downwards from thereon in; and it was also SATs year - more stress. Throughout my life, I have always had high expectations of myself, and whenever I fail to meet them, I tend to break down. I have only ever wanted to make Mum proud, and over the years I have felt that I have let myself and my family down. I have had some great moments, which will come up later in my story, but overall, I am disappointed I haven't been able to reach my full potential.

This was truly the year to forget. I started to develop feelings for a Colombian girl. The funny thing is, throughout the whole situation, and even in the latter years of school, we got on quite well. I remember on an adventure week in sixth form, we were put in the same team, and we were immensely supportive of each other. I feel this whole situation was a huge misunderstanding, and with the 'two table' gangs, it just spiralled out of control.

Throughout Year 9 my feelings grew for her and I again made the stupid mistake of telling someone about it. Inevitably, it spread around, and again it was used against me for a long time. I never wanted any of this, but it got more and more absurd the more time passed. Looking back, although I wasn't completely innocent, I actually didn't do much wrong. I was a naive 13-year-old boy who didn't understand any of the social rules involved in 'liking girls', so I became a little obsessive; and I was also still trying to come to grips with things like eye contact, which is normal to everyone else.

Having said that, I never did anything to intentionally hurt or upset her, and instead it was continuous peer pressure across the two tables which I feel made her snap and do something that haunts me to this day. Something she never knew was just how backstabbing and two-faced her friends were and throughout everything I always defended her.

It was silly things like people writing, 'I love you' on an orange and passing it to her from one table to the other. I think that was the worst thing, that we were always in close proximity having to deal with it constantly. It got to a point where she lost it and, from what I was told, she and ZS designed a death-threat note by cutting letters from a magazine and gave it to me.

That was the moment I truly broke down. I was dealing with moving home; mum and Justin splitting up; the torrent of abuse, both inside and outside of school; and still having no idea why I was like I was, and not receiving any form of support. I was unable to defend myself, express myself, or do anything to stop everything that had happened.

And here's where we reach one of the lowest points of my life, something I haven't revealed until now: In 2002, I tried to take my own life.

It wasn't by a conventional method - I was a young boy and just wanted to stop hurting. What I did was place a pillow over my own head and tried to suffocate myself. I know now this isn't possible, but the intent was there. After about a minute I stopped, gasped for air, and thought to myself: *This isn't how it should end.* I thought, I don't want to do this to my family and friends who *do* care for me, and I had so much more to give.

That evening, I vowed to never to put myself in that position or to turn to such drastic measures again. Even to this day, although I have suicidal thoughts, I just could never act upon them. I know I don't deserve to suffer; I deserve to be happy just as much as anyone else, and I believe that I will find my way back into the light. I do hope my diagnosis will help me, but I won't know that until I get the support I need.

From that moment on, however, I lost all trust and confidence in myself and others and ended up doing everything with my uncles. It was my original safe space, I guess. Honestly, my family brought me back from the brink, something I will never forget.

Sadly, though, things didn't improve. One day, a few friends and I - including the usual suspects - went on a bike ride around Richmond Park. We did the usual: ice creams, climbing trees. As I've said before, I was a bit of a daredevil and proceeded to climb an old-looking tree. I was quite high up when I felt the branch weaken beneath me. In what was another clumsy moment, I plunged - from quite a height - and landed on my back, hitting my head.

The fall knocked me out, but I have no idea how long I was out cold for. I woke up, however, to my supposed friends laughing at me. After being unconscious, I couldn't believe they would do that. I think from that moment on I became more introvert, apart from with family, and unwilling to hang out with friends. This wasn't helped when I went on a trip to London with two individuals who thought it was a good idea to tell me that we were only friends because they'd placed a bet on it. Later in school, when we got a bit older, they did become reasonably good friends; but one can't forget something like that.

Back at home, things weren't improving for my siblings and Mum started seeing someone again, a guy called Paul Gayson. We also got two dogs, Bobby and Kiara. Due to my unwillingness to be around my friends anymore, I started spending a lot more time at both my nans' houses and particularly with my uncles. As mentioned before, those guys brought me back from the brink. Many of my happiest memories come from time spent with Jamie and Scott. Tee-Jay and I did everything with them, from watching TV and playing video games, to regularly going to McDonald's in Wandsworth in their car, plus lots of activities in Richmond Park including sports, bike rides and dog walks.

Year 9 ended with a trip to Disneyland Paris. It was probably when I fell in love with IW. But it just wasn't to be for her and me. I am really happy her life turned out so well though. Again, in what was a crazily organised trip, none of us slept for nearly two days as we got the coach to France, spent time at Disneyland Paris, and went back home - all in the space of around a day-and-a-half! Having said that, it was a nice end to what was a really awful year. Two great rides I remember were the Indiana Jones one, which involved a backwards roller-coaster, and Space Mountain. On my windowsill to this day, I have a Mickey Mouse teddy to remind me of that time. I have always been the sentimental type and keep memories all around my room of the better times.

Year 10 and things really didn't get better for me or my brother who I believe joined me at Elliott School. I can't recall how long he lasted at the school, but he was treated worse than I was and had to be removed and put in another school due to being bullied all the time. People must have noticed something different about my brother though as consequently he received support from teachers, family, and professionals, which led to his eventual ASD diagnosis at the age of 15. By that time, I had left Elliott and was attending South Thames College.

It was more of the same in Year 10, although now more people had turned on me due to the events of the previous year. A few did stick by me, but some saw me as this awful person, which I still don't understand. I did decide to give socialising and 'getting out there' another go eventually and did so mainly by seeing BP and KA. Honestly, KA made my life a bit more bearable. I regularly went to Southfields to his house, sometimes with other friends; and we had regular visits to Riley's pool bar, including going to this amazing baguette place afterwards, trips to Wimbledon Park and even the odd

Wimbledon tennis tournament. I think it was around this time I discovered a love for tennis. American, Andy Roddick was a particular favourite; he had such a powerful serve. We also played football in Wandsworth Park, which became a tradition. There were kids from our year, the year below and the year above, and I honestly had some of the best times of my life there.

But things took another turn for the worse during my final years at Elliott. I was mugged three times, which is more reason for me to fear the world. The first time, the guys and I were walking home from school and a bunch of bigger kids with bikes stopped us. Instinctively, everyone ran off and left me. Going by previous experience, I clearly wasn't capable of defending myself, so I froze, not knowing what to do. It was actually a pathetic mugging. They stole £2 and my bus pass. The second occasion was closer to home, on Danebury Avenue. VS and I were walking home past the chip shop when once again we were mugged by a bunch of bigger kids. The third time I believe I was on the way to the Alton Club, when I was stopped by some bigger kids who, 'needed money for Greggs'. Of course, I gave them the money because, as mentioned before, I hate confrontation or arguments. All three incidents had a massive effect on me and further broke me mentally.

I might have entertained ambitions of being a police officer around this time, but I certainly did try something new to distract me from all that was happening in my life.

My mum's friend, known as Beefy, ran a kickboxing class at Putney Leisure Centre and I decided to give it a go. I needed to keep myself busy, develop my fitness and strength, and predominantly learn to defend myself. I lasted for a while but never gained any belts. I had one of the hardest front-under kicks ever, according to Beefy and my classmates. It was definitely a welcome distraction from a frankly torrid time.

Two thousand and three was also the year of my first work experience. After a lot of searching, I ended up with Pete, the husband of mum's best friend Claire, working as a mechanic in Putney. On my first day, Pete told me to go get a 'long weight'. Not grasping the joke, I went to ask someone to retrieve it for him. Of course, there is no such thing, so the 'long wait' lasted close to an hour! The hours were really overwhelming but I gave it my all during my two weeks there. I came home every night exhausted and dirty from working in the garage. However, it was a good first step into the world of work.

I feel it is important to mention at this stage that I suppressed everything and never really told anyone what I was constantly dealing with. Suppression truly is a silent killer. I wish I had opened up to loved ones sooner. Although I still pushed myself to go out and see friends, I was definitely becoming more of an introvert and afraid to leave my house. My obsession at the time was with quiz shows. I used to, and still do to be fair, love to watch Challenge TV, a Sky channel constantly broadcasting quiz shows, and quiz shows on many other channels. My brother and I used to watch BBC comedy nights avidly, which were always good times.

I was starting to sense changes in my brother at this point, and over the next few years it became more difficult to be around him. I understand why, but for much of this time I felt he projected his anger and frustrations on me. As we shared a room, that became harder to handle as time went on. I promised myself from a young age, that I wanted Summer to have a good life, free from responsibilities, so I took the decision to become Tee-Jay's carer and stay with him through thick and thin.

Year 10 did have some good moments, especially doing stuff with TP and RH. We attended Chelsea and Fulham matches (I even went to see Fulham play in Birmingham on two separate occasions), had days up in London, and I stayed at TP's house a lot. I have good and bad memories of going there, but I'm glad to say mostly positive. Even though we have drifted apart over the years, I am still close with his sister CP who is, by a weird coincidence, a long-term friend of Tee-Jay's.

I used to love going to TP's after a day out somewhere, and we would spend all-nighters playing Football Manager and a Star Wars game we once completed in one night. Groups of us used to stay at his too, and one morning in 2003 we woke up early to watch England win the Rugby World Cup in Australia.

Some of those nights and outings I will never forget; however, there was also one occasion I remember for the wrong reasons.

Out of respect, I will not go into the details, but Years 10 and 11 were when I had one of my last major crushes at Elliott when I fell for NM. Let's just say TP betrayed my trust because he knew how I felt about her and did something that was hard to forgive.

To finish on a plus - in a sense - we as a group once spent a whole day together, starting out at Chessington Zoo before enjoying a late one up in Central London - which honestly terrified me - before heading back for a midnight screening of Star Wars: Episode II - Attack of the Clones in the cinema. It was a crazy day, and when Mum got wind of it, she ended up grounding me for a month, which I thought was excessive.

Over the course of my life, I have developed a serious fear of fireworks: I have nearly been severely injured - or worse - on *four* occasions. The first, and worst, occurred in school. Believe it or not, I was sitting having my packed lunch while everyone else was in the dinner line, picking up their food. Out of nowhere, a kid hurtled down the stairs and threw a firework underneath my table. People were shouting for me to move and run away but I thought they were messing about. I had just got up to walk towards them when I heard an explosion behind me. I was only just out of range and could have been seriously hurt. The second occasion was when I was out with my uncles. They lit a firework that had a delayed take-off. It shot up about 3 feet into the air before exploding and nearly hitting all of us. The third incident was on a night out at a fun fair near Craven Cottage, Fulham. Towards the end of the night, a fireworks display got going. During the display, one firework diverted right towards me and exploded on the floor next to me. The last episode was actually in the safety of my own garden. This was the weirdest one. We were at my nan's and having a traditional firework display. I think it was Paul who inadvertently put a firework at an angle. It went off, ricocheted off a fence, glanced off a back wall, and screamed back towards the garden door where I was standing. I ducked just in time and the firework landed on the couch, setting it on fire. From then on, I just haven't trusted them, so mostly watch displays on TV.

While I was in Year 10, that little known film Love Actually, was filmed at the school. Several scenes were shot at Elliott, including Olivia Olson, who played Joanna in the movie, singing All I Want For Christmas Is You in the sixth form assembly hall, and Claudia Schiffer being filmed in my old history corridor. I was devastated not being chosen to be an extra in the movie, although I think the school made the decision, drawing names from a hat. It is still funny seeing some of my friends in the movie, albeit very briefly, and even now it is still a movie I love.

The final year before sixth form had the added stress of it being GCSE year. By this point, I had almost given up on most of my peers, and preferred spending time with my uncles. I have some great memories. But I especially loved the bike rides around Richmond Park. My brother and I had our fair share of crashes but flying down those hills was such a stress reliever. Feeling the wind in my face and hurtling around the park during the day and after dark surrounded by silence was just an amazing feeling. Nan was also incredible during my time at Elliott, helping me so much in my studies, which I will never forget.

This was the year my final sibling on my mum's side was born. Isabelle Ball, born on 20th February 2004, is Paul and Mum's only baby. This was also the time we got to know the Reillys, Paul Gayson's family, our extended family, a bit better. I absolutely adore Donna, Glen, Shannon and Britney who have each, in their own way, been wonderful to me, particularly in recent years. Despite them being Izzie's family, I consider them to be mine too.

So good times, but bad too. RV made sure of that. During a GCSE PE lesson in the sports hall during a gymnastics session, he sneaked up behind me and pulled my pants down. A few, including a shocked EP, turned around and saw me red-faced and stunned. As if he hadn't done enough many times over the years, he again made me feel like nothing.

The last time I saw him was prom night at the end of Year 11. What started as a lovely day, where we were presented with awards and celebrated the end of KS4, took a turn for the worse. We'd got on a bus, probably to Clapham Common; I'm not too clear. Already out of my comfort zone, I had decided to go along because it might be the last time I'd see some of these kids. At this point RV was with IW but on prom night he decided to cheat on her with another girl. I saw what he'd done, and I asked friends if I should tell IW. But I just couldn't bring myself to rat on him, and honestly, I wanted to declare my love for her that evening! But I froze, and anxiety got the better of me yet again. Despite also liking LL in my final school year, it was always about one person. The kicker was that at the end of the evening, I had only those two to go home with. I was absolutely devastated as I parted ways with her, and she was none the wiser. The worst thing was that a year before, RV had told me in Powell Park, near Richmond Park, that I could have her as he didn't want to be with her after I'd told him how I felt about IW. It's just so hard to forgive what all these people put me through, and although it did calm down in the sixth form, my time at Elliott is crammed with things I wish I could forget.

To end this horrible chapter of my life, let's mention GCSEs. Typically, and knowing my luck, as the exam period started, I was struck down with gastroenteritis. I still had to attend my exams, which were arduous and a lot to deal with on top of all my other issues. In the end, I was quite proud of the results I achieved. After I got them, and knowing I had the grades to go on to further education, I decided to stay on for the sixth form at Elliott. Despite hating most of my time there, I wasn't ready to go through another change of environment and starting again, making new friends in a new school.

So, I stayed on with some of the better people I met, although some of the mean ones remained too. All in all, prior to sixth form, there weren't many positives from my time at Elliott School.

A bowling outing in Kingston with more friends from school. Probably someone's birthday.

Elliott Year 9 awards with some good - and some not so good - friends.

CHAPTER 5

A-LEVELS AND SOUTH THAMES COLLEGE

AROUND this time, we moved home again, from Ibsley Gardens to Danebury Avenue. We had come full circle because it's where my life began. Amazingly, we even got a home next door to my nan. For the next few years this proved hugely beneficial for my siblings and I. Tee-Jay made good friends - one of his closest - with Lucas, a boy who lived the other side of Nan. Tee-Jay had had a very difficult time too, including a similarly bad time at Elliott. It got so bad that Mum had to take him out of that school and place him in an all-boys school. For a while, things seemed to improve before it all started to happen again. Like me, Tee-Jay was quiet and socially isolated at school. Unlike Elliott, the all-boys school spotted quite early on that he was struggling socially and suggested he be referred for an ASD assessment. Since being officially diagnosed, he has had a lot more support, which helped him to finish college and university. From that moment, when he was 15 and diagnosed, my mum and I have been his joint carers, helping him lead his best life.

Looking back, I feel this is the point where I potentially could have gone under the radar. I stuck with Elliott, and they never really identified any of my difficulties. I didn't really know there *was* anything wrong with me at this point. I thought I was just a teenager enduring a lot of bad luck, just in the wrong school in the wrong town. By this time, Summer was progressing nicely. She developed a great passion for dancing in her later years at primary school. I went to watch her do ballet from time to time.

Sixth form, and some faces had left, moved on to college or jobs, and some had stayed on at Elliott. We also got a number of new additions, among them VS, FS, SC and SP. Earlier in the year, after receiving my results, I decided to continue my studies in Spanish and Maths; they were my two favourite subjects. However, I also wanted a new challenge so gave Economics and Biology a try. Honestly, I lasted about two lessons in each before I switched to Psychology. But the same happened again:

I discovered the significant increase in level from KS4 to KS5 and it took me by surprise. I changed one more time, giving Physics a go this time, and had to stick with it until the end of the year. In the end, I settled for Spanish, Physics and Maths.

I always loved my Spanish lessons with Mr J. The most amazing thing was that only VS and I were the class; just two of us. Consequently, we were able to get much more support and help in our studies. I think it's also where I started liking VS; we had similar interests and spent a lot of time together. Mr J was a great teacher who was so laid back but excellent at what he did. We did also have an out-of-class teacher, Miss M, who was a beautiful lady, and really good at developing my language.

Another wonderful thing about these couple of years is that we got to make friends with both the years above and below us. They ended up joining us in what became the traditional Wandsworth Park football match, as well as numerous outings. One girl in particular was OC. Unaware at the time she was seeing someone else (they are still together today), she was the last girl I had strong feelings for at Elliott. She and her partner are, and always will be, dear friends of mine. I used to love having tennis sessions with her at Dover House Road. As a really good footballer herself, she regularly made an appearance at Wandsworth Park. I met some of my favourite people through football, such as AM, AL, SB, AH, OS and GG among many.

I still went quite often to places like Southfields and the pool club, as well as KA's house, but also gave some after school clubs a try too. Ever willing to try new things, I regularly attended an after-school debate club where guests came in and shared their stories. I also attended indoor football sessions, which were so much fun and a great way to end the week. While we were playing indoor football one day, a boy called Dennis was in possession of the ball and I proceeded to intercept it. He, being a larger and stronger player, absorbed my pressure and thrust me full force into a wall. I broke my arm in three places. It was, and still is, my only broken bone, but at the time I was unaware of how bad the damage was. So, I got changed, left school, and hopped on the bus by myself in absolute agony. I got home and Mum immediately took me to the hospital. The doctors fit me with a plaster cast, and I was stuck in it for six weeks. To make matters worse, it was my writing hand, so I needed help with writing notes and doing homework. The school said I could sue, but in all honesty, it was just an accident.

Coming from a dark place in previous years, I once again tried to become more active and social again. I continued to go to the places where I felt most comfortable, mainly Waterloo or Kingston, with friends, although my anxiety with public transport had definitely got worse. I even had to force myself to go to an end-of-year party at Putney Rowing Club. I was terrified and honestly pretty much sat in the same spot the entire night. Luckily, I had company in the shape of SC, who became one of my closer friends and formed part of the trio of KH, RH and SC.

It wasn't all plain sailing. I still didn't look forward to lunch times and free periods because some people were still making it increasingly difficult for me, not understanding the state I was in. Some of the familiar faces from secondary school were still around, making school life unbearable still at times. As mentioned before, A-levels overwhelmed me and were a massive step up from GCSEs, and I didn't achieve the greatest results in first year, aside from a decent Spanish grade. Nonetheless, I kept plugging away and did get a few better results in the second year, achieving an A-level in Spanish and AS in Maths. I gave Film a try in the second year but, like Biology, Economics and Psychology, it proved a step too far.

My favourite time in sixth form was an adventure week in the Lake District as part of Outward Bound. I overcame some big fears during this week, especially my fear of heights. A brief spell also occurred when everyone was kind and supportive towards me. Even the ones who had done me wrong in previous years were helpful, particularly as the activities increased in difficulty. We all had to be up at 6am to go for a jog to a nearby lake. Then, one by one, we had to jump into the ice-cold water, which really did wake us up and prepare us for the day. There were plenty of activities, some as an individual and some as a team. Team-building exercises included building a raft that would get around eight of us across the lake without sinking. We just about made it.

The high ropes were a big challenge. And we had to climb this ridiculously thin pole before standing atop it and, while it wobbled side-to-side, make a leap of faith to a swinging bar some distance away. Gorge walking was fun. You climbed upstream in your wet suit, clambering over all sorts of obstacles, under impediments, navigating the water, before this massive jump at the end. Some people couldn't take the plunge, but I did. And jumping in, I felt like the depth of it was never ending. Not the strongest of swimmers, I had to quickly get back to the surface.

I gained a lot of confidence during this week, so much so that I pushed myself to tell SC that I loved her as a friend; something I could never have done normally. I walked with her to a nearby hill and went on about how much I appreciated and valued our friendship.

Some of the activities felt like being in I'm a Celebrity, Get Me Out of Here... particularly one involving a maze, utter darkness and a torch on your helmet. This was another big challenge but with wonderful support from my group I made it through. We also took part in zip-lining, climbing, abseiling, and lots of other really fun activities.

This leads me to one of my proudest achievements to date. In 2005, as part of a group, I climbed Helvellyn, the third highest mountain in England. It was an incredible feat. It was a wonderful feeling being at one with nature and the first time I realised I would love to travel at some point and enjoy similar experiences to this. After what seemed like an eternity, we arrived at this plateau just before reaching the summit. We set up camp, cooked food and fetched and filtered water from a little stream. It was a surreal feeling I hadn't experienced before, sleeping under the stars and outdoors generally; but it's another memory that sticks in my mind. The following morning, we woke up to the sound of nature. Opening my tent, I saw an animal, which I think might have been a goat, making lots of noise - another new experience. And this is where it got crazy. For the final ascent, we had to climb up this rocky mountain face with no safety gear. To this day, I have no idea how we were allowed to do this. We obviously all made it safely and I was so happy to have achieved this, that I ran to the top to be the first to complete this amazing feat. This was a truly unforgettable experience and in the top five of my proudest moments.

Year 2 of 6th form, and what turned out to be my final year at Elliott, was honestly a little quieter. It was mostly more of the same at school, more memories made with my uncles, and me continuing to try find my way back from where I was by being more active and sociable. Strangely, one of the first things that comes to mind from this year was a detention. It had been a long journey through Elliott school days, and sixth form was no exception. We had all worked incredibly hard and one day decided to play football during our free period. We were supposed to be studying and preparing for exams, and the head of Sixth was having none of it. So, there we were, outside having a break from our studies, when out stormed Mr T, screaming at us. Everybody ran for their lives, except for one person. Although I started to run, I realised very quickly there was absolutely no point - he knew the lot of us. So, I stopped; froze. As I've said, I don't like being in anyone's bad books, so this deeply upset me. In the end, he caught everyone involved and we were all put in detention. Thus, The EWMS (Elliott Working Man's Society) was born.

A post-millennium Breakfast Club, we formed a group that lasted until the end of our time at Elliott. It actually got very popular, as members put up posters and flyers promoting it almost like an extracurricular activity. We played cards, particularly a game called Kempf. It slowly evolved from detention into a social club. So much so that students who didn't get detention even started to join us! I think pupils even wrote a song for it to the tune of Getta Bloomin' Move On! (The Self Preservation Society) featured in the movie, The Italian Job. What began as detention, something terrifying because I didn't like being in trouble, quickly became a social event that I enjoyed.

I had dreaded the oral part of my final Spanish exam all year. It involved having a fluent conversation for 10 minutes with Mr J. Somehow, I got through it and was really proud of myself.

Walking down the hallway to see my friend in the library, I came across students playing truth or dare. The dare was for a girl called Cassie to kiss the next person who crossed her path. It happened to be me. Elated from just doing well in my exam, and in a crazy moment, I agreed to do it. In what was a kiss that was supposed to last a few seconds ended up being for much longer. It was really out of character for me, but she was a beautiful girl, and I was on a high after my exam. It was a nice way to end a very difficult, few years.

However pleasant that experience was, I was really struggling with everything that was happening around me; but I kept going, particularly with my Spanish which I always enjoyed. Having failed Physics, I had just the two subjects that year — Spanish and Maths. A-Levels were an overwhelming challenge, so I was proud to get one A-Level and one AS at the end of it. But it was nowhere near enough to continue on to university. I was at a crossroads.

Strangely, despite the difficulties throughout Elliott, part of me didn't want it to end. I almost felt accustomed to coming to school practically every day for the last seven years. I was never good with change, and this was a big one in terms of either entering the world of work or continuing at another college. Another option was another year at Elliott, but the courses were limited and not what I was looking for. This is when I went to see Mr H to decide what to do next. As my love of sports, particularly tennis, was growing, I decided after a long chat that I wanted to do a sports course, which wasn't available at Elliott. Mr H suggested I go to South Thames College on Putney Hill, which was about a 10-minute walk from school. After some deliberation I thought it was time to move on; I couldn't stay there forever. At this time, I wanted to work in the sports industry, in an outdoor environment and with children, so for me the logical step was to become a tennis coach. As I had finished my final year way short of the requirements to get into university, I opted for South Thames College where I would study BTEC Sports Development and Fitness to secure the UCAS points required. This was an opportunity for a fresh start; another chance to reach my true potential.

September 2006, I was on my new path, studying at South Thames. Although not on the same course as me, there were a couple of familiar faces at the college. VS and CP also came to study there. I took to the course quickly, as I now had an incentive and a greater idea of what I wanted to do. I even had some wonderful classmates, including HE, DF, CF, JB, RE, SC and many others who made these two years particularly memorable. The almost inevitable anxiety and fear lingered but dissipated quite quickly as I was welcomed by staff and students. My trust and confidence were really low though due to the previous part of my life. I had immense trust issues and struggled to befriend others; and honestly, outside of class, I barely recall doing anything with any of my friends. Unlike at Elliott, I actually loved lunchtime. There was a common room supervised by a relative of one of my dear friends, TB. The supervisors, MB and KK, made those times really enjoyable. The common room was a great break from my studies and almost reminded me of a youth club/play centre with the activities they provided.

Despite taking well to this new chapter of my life, part of me just couldn't leave Elliott school behind. So, in first year I occasionally popped back to see some teachers and friends from the year below. As I've mentioned, I grow attachments to people and things, and I really struggle letting them go. It's always been the case.

After college, I sometimes went back to Elliott to play indoor football, which I always enjoyed greatly. I even got to see KH's sister, which was really nice. I remember once, on my way home from college, bumping into my former adversary, JM. He had changed so much; I was astounded. But I could not forget what he had put me through. It was a brief catch up and we continued on our respective paths.

Once again it was apparent: I was the goody two-shoes and the quiet one of the class and it was clear early on that I was the go-to guy to help others in their studies. I was initially struggling to fit in again, but this gave me an opportunity to become better friends with certain people. It was a laid-back course, and the afternoons were particularly great: three days a week we enjoyed a two-hour indoor football session. A fond memory we'll never forget. It also gave me a chance to improve my fitness ahead of what was to come in the following year. Alongside this course, I also decided to undertake an evening course to hone my coaching skills and potentially open more doors in the leisure industry. My teachers were great at South Thames. Mr M in particular was always so supportive and helpful.

But it wasn't all great. I suffered my first family loss that year. Grandpa Ron was in hospital. Izzie was just two at the time. We went to visit him to say goodbye. It sounds cliché but I think he waited for us all to arrive so he could bid farewell before passing. I'm generally awful around death but I can't really envisage a better way to go; surrounded by family.

Two thousand and six was my 18th birthday. Being an introvert, full of anxiety and not enjoying being in groups, having a big party was really not my kind of thing. Nonetheless, I was aware that this was a significant milestone in any person's life, and it was also an opportunity to see friends and family, some of whom I'd not seen in a few years. The event took place in a local club close to Dover House Road. As you would expect, there was a lot of peer pressure that night. Having never been drunk before it was an opportunity for people to see me under the influence. I was pressured into downing pints and numerous other drinks, which, to this day, I really don't like. I have never enjoyed the taste of alcohol. I guess you could say the rest of the night was a blur, but I do remember getting home, feeling very unwell and, the next morning, waking up with a massive hangover. It was nice to see so many familiar faces, but partying is not something I took to as I got older. I've never really been a party goer or drinker. So, I definitely felt out of my comfort zone. Neither do I enjoy being the centre of attention. That feeling where you stand there while people sing Happy Birthday, or you have to deliver a speech, for example: I just cannot handle it. But I guess it was a memorable night one way or another.

My timeline may be a little off, but this is around the time my mum and Paul split up. The following year she started seeing her boss, John O'Connell. That year too, 2007, I got my first jobs. The first was working voluntarily with my mum and John at Heathside Day Centre, Roehampton, which was just across the road from my old primary school. It was my mum's first real foray into the world of mental health. I spent a few hours a week there, one or two days, outside my studies. For six months - June 2007 to January 2008 - I worked voluntarily, building relationships with adults recovering from mental health problems and encouraging participation in group activities. We played pool, went bowling and played football with the members. It was also where I met a true family friend, Shaun Little. He has also been with us through thick and thin. I found this role very fulfilling; it gave me an escape from everything and was a welcome distraction from my studies.

I also did some voluntary work at the Bank of England Sports Centre in Roehampton to help me with my ambition of becoming a tennis coach. For almost three years, over two spells, I volunteered as an assistant coach working with children aged four to 12.

These were becoming a very strenuous two years. But I didn't stop pushing myself. In 2007 I decided to run the Silverstone Half Marathon for charity. As well as UCAS applications, completing my Level 1 coaching badge in tennis, family responsibilities and finishing up at South Thames, this was another proud moment. After months of training at the college gym, afternoon and after-college football and bike rides with my uncles, I was ready to do this.

Race day was challenging. My motion sickness made the drive there and back tough and the weather was also horrendous: windy, heavy rain. To this day, I still have no idea how I crossed the finish line because I injured my leg on the first corner. It was so painful, but I was determined to keep going. Neither gusts of wind, sheets of rain, the 13.1 miles, 'the wall', nor a leg injury stopped me! I ploughed on, sprinting the final 100 meters. It was such an incredible feeling as I crossed the line and received my medal, one I have never forgotten.

After the event, we went to Aylesbury to visit Granny Kath. I could not move my legs for the following few days and sat in Granny's living room unable to budge, absolutely exhausted from what I had just been through.

Heading towards the end of my time at South Thames, I had reached another fork in the road. Where next? I had finished my UCAS applications but wasn't sure if further education was for me. I had achieved a distinction merit in my course (another achievement I took great pride in) so had the right amount to continue my educational journey. Do I go all in with tennis coaching? Do I go to Roehampton University? Do I look for work elsewhere? Turned out to be none of these in the end. Instead, I decided to take a massive leap of faith and undertake the Camp America experience.

Because this was so out of my comfort zone, I spent six months preparing myself. Work at the Bank of England Sport Centre helped. After completing my Level 1 tennis coaching, I volunteered to work with children under the leadership of JE, MM and AK. I studied drills and ways to keep varying the sessions to keep the kids entertained. This was pivotal as at Camp

America I became a tennis coach and camp counsellor to ten 13-year-old-boys. Prior to going, I took a First Aid course at the National Tennis Centre, next door to the Bank of England Sports Centre. They played Wimbledon qualifiers there and some of the best players used the courts to practice. I was waiting for my course to commence when a certain Andy Murray walked past me and out onto the clay courts. Having not met anyone famous before I naturally froze; I had a bit of a star-struck moment. Then I pulled myself together, thought, *This is probably the only time you will ever get to meet him,* jumped off my seat, and ran out to greet him. It was a really nice moment and although I had an outdated phone, I got a photo with him. I pushed through the anxiety barrier and instinctively went to speak to him, which was a big thing personally. Just to add to what was already a crazy day, after the course finished, I popped through the centre to go and see my work colleagues next door. On my way, I saw former British tennis stars Tim Henman and Greg Rusedski having lunch. Quite a surreal feeling and one I will always remember.

Before my Camp America experience, I also had to push myself to get over my anxiety regarding public transport and new environments. I had to go to the US Embassy to apply for my visa, attend an interview and open day, all in Central London, to see what camp I would be going to and if I was what they were looking for. Then came the preparation for what was another significant part of my life.

At Stamford Bridge, Chelsea.

Outward bound in the Lake District.

At the peak of Helvellyn in the Lake District.

Family photo when we moved back to Danebury Avenue.

CHAPTER 6

THE LEAP OF FAITH, FWF 2000 AND GREAT, TENNIS, TY AND DISNEYWORLD

AS YOU can see, I had definitely got back into a place where I felt content in my life, although there was still a lot going on. South Thames and all I had achieved in recent years had given me a new found confidence to take anything on, head on. In the summer of 2008, this was truly realized by one of the most significant periods of my life happening, Camp America. After passing the interview stage, getting my visa, selecting my camp and preparing myself for the summer ahead, it started to become all too real. I took to social media to find others in the same boat and gain some advice and guidance on the adventure we were about to embark on.

This is where I met a few truly wonderful people: DU, LA, EH, AL, GH, AH, TH, CB and HL. DU was the first one I really spoke to. She was a wonderful girl from Liverpool who was heading out to the States to teach dance. We clicked quite early on and really helped put each other at ease in the months prior to our flight to New York.

As the time got closer, we joined a group who were also on our flight, making this part a bit more bearable. I was absolutely petrified heading to the airport and leaving my mum behind. I was really hesitant to put my suitcase on the conveyor belt and head through the door to Departures because it would be almost three months before I saw my family again. It wasn't until I got to boarding, until I saw some of the others, and until I saw DU's face, that I started to feel better. But I was still genuinely frightened. I had never been on a plane before. My anxiety hit new levels as we took off and headed to New York's JFK Airport.

After a six-hour flight, and another horrible case of motion sickness, we landed safely, and all headed to the exit to be greeted by a representative of French Woods Festival of The Performing Arts. Upon leaving the airport and heading into the city, I started to compare what I was seeing with what I'd seen on TV. It started with all the yellow taxis, then a news stand featuring the New York Times newspaper.

We had a pit stop about halfway into the journey and got some food and drinks. I bought myself the most incredible giant pretzel, and what was to be the first of an immense number of Mountain Dew drinks!

After about an hour's drive, we turned into what was going to be our home for the next 12 weeks or so. French Woods is a wonderful camp based in the Catskill Mountains in New York State. It is a performing arts camp and is full of young talent aspiring to achieve in fields such as theatre, music and circus; but it also provided many activities to keep the campers happy during a three-month summer stay. We were shown to our cabins and introduced to fellow counsellors and the campers we'd be responsible for. We got the first day or so to ourselves to recover from jet lag, explore our new surroundings and become acclimatised to life in the USA.

After unpacking and getting some rest, I reunited with my group, and we had our first look around. The most beautiful view was the lake front, which was right next to our cabin. It was an incredible summer camp. It had everything, including a fully-fledged circus department, grand theatre stages for the children to perform, a number of tennis courts, a baseball field, magic department, rock shop - where you could learn to play instruments - and arts and crafts, among many other activities.

The first day, we strolled around the lake and came across a haunted house. Well, it looked like a haunted house, abandoned and rustic. We looked like the cast of Scooby-Doo walking up to it, as if we expected some ghost to scold us for being "pesky kids". When we got back, we went for our first dinner with our respective campers and counsellors. The following morning, we woke up to The Beatles' song Here Comes the Sun, and something we were not used to, the raising of the American flag, which took place every morning.

The second day, still on edge and struggling to adapt, I, with a few of my new friends, tried out a few of the activities available at French Woods. I headed for the tennis courts and gave a short coaching session to DU, TH, GH and HL. That day I met the wonderful LA who was teaching fencing. She played a big part in getting me though the first week.

I was also introduced to my fellow tennis coaches, who included JV and his sister JV, and TK, DP, LM and OR. This was also the day I met the person who was to become the love of my life, AS (Ty). Ty was a beautiful person inside and out and had a very interesting background. She was adopted at a young age, I believe, and only met her biological father once. He was a monk who took a vow to meet his daughter only once before committing completely to his orders.

Although she was originally from Thailand, Ty lived in the Netherlands. She spoke five languages and, like all the tennis coaches, was on another level in terms of her tennis ability. At this point I was at a pretty decent level; however, seeing them play showed me how far I had to go to be a top player.

In what was another naïve moment, which I will always regret, I naturally thought that when seeking a potential girlfriend while in the States, I had to find someone from my own country. As a result, I firstly developed a big crush on DU and then later on with another now friend for life, RS. The best friends I met at camp were general counsellors such as MK, SD, RS, SS, and some others, who became family. I am happy to say I'm still in contact with several of them today.

A typical day at camp consisted of an early wake up and breakfast in the canteen before the children went off to their respective activities. I was on court about six hours each day in 30-plus degree heat. We had a drinks machine nearby where I bought my daily Mountain Dew. After the first three activities we had lunch, then the afternoon sessions got going. We did get one free period when we could do what we wanted: rest up, use the computer (with awful internet connection), take clothes to the laundromat or take part in some of the activities ourselves. Then we would meet back at the cabin before heading for dinner, after which we had to prepare for the evening activity, which mostly consisted of watching the amazingly talented kids performing in shows and musicals. After the show, there was a period of free time when pizza and these amazing milkshakes were provided, before we headed back to the cabins.

It was a rotation policy with regards to who looked after - or babysat - the kids, and sometimes a counsellor in training was given this dubious honour. It's no picnic telling ten 13-year-olds to get to bed. They're not always good listeners - especially if you're only about seven years older than them. Once they had gone to bed we had the rest of the night to ourselves. We mostly sat in the common room just hanging out with each other. There was another option offsite, known as the Country Club (CC), which was a place people went to have fun and socialize. I only went there once, on the final evening, because it was, again, very out of my comfort zone, and I was also exhausted after a hard day's work. Another rotational duty was guarding the respective departments, because young teens liked to break curfew and get up to mischief. They were busy and hectic days but truly memorable.

I absolutely loved teaching the kids tennis and working with such wonderful colleagues. It was exhausting, and honestly, their standard, for the most part, was better than mine; but it was such a joy to be a part of. And I even got to teach Will Smith's nephew tennis! Other mentionable names include CF, MH, AK, SA and JD, among many, many amazing people.

We also got to have so-called "lazy days": one day free for staff every two weeks (if I remember right). On the days we had to ourselves, we could go on excursions, stay at camp, or chaperone the kids to the cinema. I did a bit of everything, trying to make the most of my American adventure. A couple of times I went to the cinema with Ty and the kids and saw Mamma Mia and Get Smart. I will never forget how much fun I had watching both these films with Ty, and how cheesy we found Mamma Mia. The cinema, based in the small town of Hancock, was hired out for use by the camp. It had two screens, so we had a choice of movie each time we went.

There was also a day trip to a nearby mall, a trip to a Six Flags theme park and a day in Philadelphia. The trip to Six Flags started badly. It was probably the only day during my time in America that we endured torrential rain. However, the FW family and I still made the most of what was an amazing day out, and it was a welcome change from the day-to-day camp experience. Philadelphia was the first day I spent with my Aussie friend BT. I feel that was the day we formed a great bond. If it weren't for her, I think I would have got lost and not made it back to the coach on time. We saw the Liberty Bell, the famous symbol of American independence, went shopping and wandered the streets exploring, gaining further experience of US culture. I loved it when we met up with the FW family and stopped for lunch at a really amazing restaurant. All in all, it was a really nice day.

One evening, JB, JM, RR and I were taking care of the kids before the counsellor-in-training came. The kids decided to pull a prank. They dressed in robes, painted a pentagram on the floor, switched all lights off, and lit candles to make it look like a sort of altar where a cult gathered for sacrifice. Needless to say, AK came in and was really freaked out; but it was really funny.

After a few weeks of adjusting to America, a special holiday arrived - Independence Day. This was a day when the English counsellors were treated differently from the off and counsellors from different countries had to perform in front of the others. The day began with us being abruptly woken at 6am, forced out of bed and outside by our campers and taken to the waterfront. We were lined up in single file and made to jump in the ice-cold lake. As with Outward Bound, jumping into an ice-cold lake really does wake you up! In the week leading up to Independence Day, the English contingent created props and shirts for us all to wear. Our performance, led by the lovely SS, was Harry Potter and the Cursed Camp. A number of the English counsellors had written a script and we performed on behalf of our nation, although most of us, including me, just stood in the background. It all ended with an England v. The Rest of the World football match. I really enjoyed it; even got the opening goal with a well taken header. We won it 4-2. It was an unusual day, where I got to see patriotism displayed unlike any I'd seen before.

There were a number of themed days like this in my time at camp, but one stood out in particular: Carnival Day. In front of each cabin there was a game or activity, and in the middle of it all, was a massive Slip 'N Slide. I remember there being a Gladiator-type activity in which we had duelling equipment and had to knock each other off a beam. There was face painting and fun fair games, like the one where you hit a target and a person falls into a pool of water. I really liked DU at this point, but it was also when I started to like RS. It was another fun day that we all enjoyed.

One of the highlights of my time at camp was when, out of nowhere, the band Maroon 5 came to visit. We were just having lunch when all of a sudden, there was Adam Levine and the band! It turns out, French Woods was where the band formed and were good friends with the owners of the camp. They stayed throughout the day and even performed some of their songs, which was incredible. It was a truly special place and an environment where people became family in a short space of time.

But it wasn't all sun and smiles though. It was actually a lot of hard work and an exhausting experience. While I was coaching one day, Ty fainted due to the heat and intensity of her efforts. They took her to the medical suite where she regained consciousness and was thankfully okay. I was naturally terrified seeing her collapse, and I thought that with the amount of concern shown, I was falling in love with her. I still had feelings for RS, but Ty was logically the one I should have been with, despite her living in Amsterdam.

One evening when I was guarding the circus department, I experienced a moment that broke my heart. I saw RS with another guy, walking off into the distance. I sat on one of the landing mats and thought to myself, *Not again.* I had a meltdown and bawled my eyes out for such a long time. I started to feel homesick and wanted to go home. RS returned a while later and saw me struggling. The rest is a bit of a blur, but it was a painful moment. At this point I want to say RS is now married, has children and will be a friend for life. I'm just telling my story the only way I know how.

From that moment on, I only had eyes for one. Ty was the most wonderful person I have ever known and was my first proper date. Towards the end of camp, we had an event called Banquet when we all came together and had a celebratory evening with food and fun. At the end of the evening, we went to the common room and enjoyed each other's company, lying on the couch, watching TV. She was the best thing that ever happened to me, which made the final week so difficult. It had been a wonderful and life-changing summer, and although the pay wasn't great, I would recommend it to anyone.

The final evening was one of the hardest nights ever. We went to the Country Club to celebrate a wonderful summer. As always, I failed to fit in and felt out of place, so I headed back. Ty was feeling unwell and hadn't gone so I wanted to go see her. In what was planned to be the night I told her how I felt, I knocked on her cabin door. Devastatingly, there was no answer. After a couple of attempts I headed to bed. The next morning was our last at camp and little did I know, at the time, the last time I would ever see Ty.

In the week leading up to this day I was fully prepared to go home. However, I was asked to come along to Disneyworld in Florida with MK, SD, AP and NB. Apparently, one of the kids' parents was offering a discount on a lovely hotel-and-park entry for a week. I had earned just under $1,000 that summer, and all of it went on having a wonderful week in Disneyworld. It was a once in a lifetime opportunity I couldn't turn down. Although fearful, I was happy with the friends I was going with, so my worries quickly dissipated. However, my thoughts were with Ty before I left for Disneyworld; I did not want to leave her. The night before, when I'd knocked on her door, she had been sleeping in the cabin next door and sadly hadn't heard me. I sometimes think to myself how life could have panned out if I'd found her and expressed my love for her that evening. Saying goodbye to that girl was the hardest thing I've ever had to do. Her bus arrived and we just embraced for around 10 minutes. I really didn't want to let her go but she had no choice.

Not in the greatest state of mind, I headed to the airport, and the five of us headed to Florida. Arriving in Orlando, we were assailed by the tremendous heat - and the Disney's Magical Express Bus. We entered our hotel complex that was surrounded by beautiful scenery and set in a stunning location. The room itself was unbelievable for the price we paid, and after unpacking we headed straight for a nearby restaurant. We had an all-inclusive deal, so it was safe to say we treated ourselves. We had the most amazing milkshakes and many lovely meals during the week.

Each day we went to a different park. Each was special in their way. We visited Magic Kingdom, Hollywood Studios, Epcot and the Animal Kingdom. The final two days were spent at Universal Studios.

At this point I need to mention the premature departure of MK, one of my favourite people from camp. He only got to experience a day or two in Florida before discovering he had a horrible infection on his leg. He had to spend the rest of the week in a local hospital. It was really sad, but SD, AP, NB and I continued on without him.

One of my funniest memories was the day in the Magic Kingdom. Having used the same flip flops for the entire summer, there was a lot of wear and tear. I was walking around when suddenly I felt a snap. The floor, at 35-degrees centigrade or higher, was absolutely scorching, and there I was, no flip flops, trying to jump to the nearest shadow, desperate to find somewhere selling shoes. I eventually came across a Croc store. Very expensive but an absolute necessity, I bought a pair of Mickey Mouse Crocs, which I still have to this day. It was a funny experience, hopping around looking for anything to put on my feet.

As mentioned earlier, I have a real fear of fireworks. Disneyworld always put on an incredible display overlooking the iconic Disney castle. Although hesitant at first, I decided to stay and see the display. And I am glad I did. It was truly incredible. There were several memorable moments from each of the four parks and Universal Studios, but as we came towards the end of the week, I was ready to go home.

My flight home was leaving from New York, so we had to fly back quite late from Florida, which led to another anxiety filled evening. Think Macaulay Culkin in the night scene from Home Alone 2: Lost in New York, and you will realise how I was feeling.

We landed at the airport and proceeded to the Subway with all our luggage. Booking a hostel in a scary part of the city was daunting, I was terrified walking the street late at night. It was all okay in the end, but I don't think I could go through that again.

The following morning, I received a call from LA, who was in a similar situation with a flight the following day. I said she could stay with us for our final evening. With a day to spare, the guys went to explore NYC. But I froze and genuinely could not leave my room. After a summer of pushing my boundaries to the limit, I just wanted to go home because New York was a truly intimidating place.

Despite having come a long way in the last few years, the underlying anxiety and fear was still there. So, the first opportunity I had, I said goodbye to everyone and went with LA to Newark Airport. I had about $2 left before boarding my flight home and after saying goodbye to LA, I went to a nearby vendor to buy a bagel and drink. Although I didn't have enough money, the lady said I could still have it, which was nice. Exhausted from recent years, I headed home to the next chapter of my life, which was no less tiring. Roehampton University, here I come.

Arriving at JFK airport in New York.

With some of the kids I taught at FWF.

Post summer fun at Disneyland in Orlando, Florida in 2008. I went there with Nathan, Simon, Adriano and Mick.

CHAPTER 7

ROEHAMPTON UNIVERSITY, GOING UNDER THE RADAR AND THE DISSERTATION FROM HELL

IT WAS at this point that I started to believe in myself again. With four years of higher education, followed by an intensive three months in America under my belt, I headed to university, ready for my next big challenge. Despite my confidence having improved recently, I was under no illusions: the next three years would be challenging. Facing the prospect again of trying to fit in, deal with a new environment and give my all to my studies, despite not being a fan of academic writing, I knew it would be tough. Keeping that balance between university, family, work and social life I knew would be difficult, but I was determined to try.

I began my degree in sport and exercise sciences in September 2008 with the ambition of becoming a tennis coach or working in the leisure industry. When I returned to London, I continued my voluntary role at the Bank of England Sports Centre. I wanted to gain further experience in tennis coaching and working with children. I once again struggled in the early weeks of university to make new friends and was starting to fear the worst once more. It was around a month into first year when I met two people who would play an integral part in getting me to the finish line. RC and BD are now two of my best friends and I am eternally grateful I met them when I did.

I realised early on just how big a step-up university was from my previous studies. The lectures were quite overwhelming and there was a lot of information to take on board. However, I did have some really nice people around to support me with my studies, both students and lecturers. The first year was probably my quietest in terms of socializing and meeting people as I was determined to get as good a grade as possible. BD on many occasions brought me out of my shell and RC, a wonderful tennis player himself, joined me in going for trials for the university teams; we both got selected for one team. My weeks were becoming more fulfilling and eventful and keeping that balance began to take its toll as the assignments started piling up.

Each week I was cycling to the Bank of England Sport Centre, making time for family and friends, new and old, and keeping up with the work, which was overwhelming enough; but this was also the year when my brother received his official ASD diagnosis and when mum and I took joint-carers responsibility for him. This, I feel, was when I went under the radar. I was developing feelings for LW, a receptionist at the tennis club, and, for a large part of the first year, a girl called Miriam. In a rare moment of confidence, I told Miriam how I felt. There were a group of guys from my class who were a bit funny in the early stages, and I could hear them mocking me after I didn't get the answer I was looking for. From previous experience, I was starting to worry it was the beginning of more mistreatment. However, I think I earned their respect that day and as our degree progressed, they became good friends, and I am still in contact with them.

I really tried to get out and try my hand at what the university had to offer, so I joined the tennis social club, which met on Fridays. This was where I met some of my favourite people from university. I even tried attending a few social events. One known as the Bop, a weekly event with different themes, and the Fez club. Honestly, it really wasn't my scene - loud music, big crowds and bright lights. But I did handle it better in the following years because I met some more wonderful people. There were also local bars such The Belfry where BD and I went to play pool and watch sports on the big screen. I even went to church once in a while to meet new people, and got to know CB, CA, EE, HB, EP and EK who are still wonderful friends of mine.

RC is one of the most committed, genuine and dedicated people I have known. Although on campus in the first year, he actually travelled down from Bicester, Oxfordshire each day there was a lecture; incredible. He put me to shame as I lived across the road from campus, and occasionally struggled to get to lectures. He came to my house each morning and we walked to our classes. I don't know how he did it, but it was evident in lectures that he was drifting off to sleep. So, the travelling must have taken its toll.

BD also really went through it at university, including renting from a nasty landlord, and going to hospital due to his poor diet. In the second year, because he was struggling with the commute from Southend, he stayed for almost an entire year with us. I loved that time, and I particularly recall playing a lot of Pro Evolution Soccer video games with him, which was a nice distraction from our studies.

The best decision I made in the first year was attending the tennis social club throughout my degree. It was a massive stress reliever and I also met AK who would introduce me to more wonderful people, who genuinely got me through to the end. I was opening doors for myself and making friends for life, and everything seemed to be on the up. To name but a few, I will be eternally grateful for AK, BO, SH, JB, SB, ZB and GM who were truly there for me, and I still miss them dearly. They provided me with so many opportunities to go university events and house visits, and on some occasions, we even went to see live TV shows being filmed. Once we went to see The Graham Norton Show being recorded. The guests were Brooke Shields, Miranda Hart, Kevin Bacon and Jedward. I will never forget these times. I feel I was becoming a more outgoing and happier person. I still felt like the quiet one but unlike previous times in my life, the "Uni family", as they became known, accepted me for me.

My confidence was high when I decided to go visit my dad and family in Cornwall. My anxiety took over quite quickly however, when I was faced with a four-and-a-half-hour trip to Truro. After dealing with the obstacle of motion sickness, I arrived, and ended up spending almost a month there, having a wonderful time. It was one of my first experiences of staying in a resort town. To this day, a resort town in England or Spain is where I would love to one day live. The first time I'd gone to Cornwall my dad had driven me there and back. But this was the first time I pushed myself to go it alone. It was lovely to see my dad, step-mum Jo and my siblings. We played tennis, went to the beach, visited town, and spent time at both Dad's and Jo's house. They each had their own place. I remember trying to catch up on the TV show *Prison Break* at her house on the computer. One of my fondest memories is when we went go-karting. Starting in last place, I did a Lewis Hamilton, overtaking everybody else on the track and ending up in first place. I also recall watching The Ashes with my dad, and that was when he told me about the time he went to Australia when I was very young. Although hard to take, I have now forgiven him and even re-added his surname to my own. It may have been the final day when Dad was taking me to the station; the sunroof was down, the wind was in our face, my siblings were in the back, and I recall *Good Riddance* by Green Day playing on the radio. I forever associate this song with my last visit to Cornwall, and whenever I hear it, I think of my family and the time I spent there.

This was the year I also pushed through some personal barriers to go and see two of my best friends from French Woods. In a moment of madness, I booked the trains to Blackburn and Liverpool. I will never forget these two weeks. I was yet again putting myself out of my comfort zone. First, I visited MK in Blackburn, which was a really great week. I met his lovely family, and we went to a local pub and met a few of his friends, and some others when we went to a sports club and played indoor football. We went to Ewood Park to see Blackburn play West Brom. Although it ended 0-0, and was a terrible game, it was a farewell appearance from Turkish midfielder, Tugay, who spent eight years at Blackburn. MK and I also went to Preston to the National Football Museum. It has since moved to Manchester. The visit to MK's wasn't all fun. I witnessed first-hand his mother's battle with MS. I knew very little about the condition, but it was truly inspiring to see how MK and his sister took care of her. MK will always be one of my favourite people. Hearing recently from him about his own troubles with mental health further inspired me to write this book.

Going to Liverpool was, for the most part, quite the opposite of my visit to Blackburn, and was a reality check that I had perhaps bitten off more than I could chew. Upon arrival at Lime Street train station, I was assailed by an anxiety attack because my friend was nowhere to be seen. I tried calling him but to no avail and was stranded. Luckily, I remembered he worked at the Revolution bar and called a taxi. There are two Revolution bars in Liverpool, so I had to guess which one SD worked at - and I guessed right. I had to wait for his shift to end before we headed back to his house. Unlike MK, SD hadn't booked the week off work, so it made for quite an uncomfortable week. I was afraid to leave the house when he wasn't there, so most of the week was spent indoors - much to his parent's surprise. We did go to the cinema, to the shopping and leisure complex Liverpool One, and visited his friends during my time there though. As wonderful as it was to see him, I really felt uncomfortable for most of my time in Liverpool.

Back home and it was a difficult time: we had lost both of our dogs, which was devastating. Grandad Colin had also seen one of the dog's lifeless body in the kitchen, which must've been awful. The other dog passed a little later, but it is something nobody should have to experience. Tee-Jay and I have always tended to be more attached to dogs than people, so this greatly affected us.

During the second year at Uni I came into my own, although my studies were becoming more overwhelming and intensive. It was the year I met the Uni family, those people I got really close to, and when I got to meet some more lovely people at social and competitive tennis events. ER was one of my better friends I made through tennis, and I used to love going to his dorm, watching football and eating this incredible duck pizza with hoisin sauce. My friends II, HS, HB, NE, BO and AK regularly came to tennis, and I think this was the year I took over as person-in-charge of social tennis. It gave me another opportunity to develop my coaching skills and just get out and play, which I loved.

I had developed feelings for some of the group at this point, including AK, CP, GM and generally HS, HB and EE. I feel at this point I just needed companionship with another person and, thinking back, it may have been peer pressure that heightened how much I liked AK. Truth be told, CP was the one I really hoped to be with. I'd had no luck in my love life so far, so after so many rejections and bad experiences, my confidence was waning, and I was convinced nobody would ever like me in that way. In the end, I just focused on my studies and working towards my eventual 2:1, which is one of my greatest achievements. Keeping the balance was getting harder, however, and I was becoming more physically and mentally exhausted.

I was finding the assignments more challenging. We had to do a presentation, which naturally petrified me. My lecturer put it down to poor writing skills, but I had plagiarised myself by recycling some previous work. I was actually unaware this was even possible. The presentation itself was hard. We had three lecturers sitting behind a table, looking like the judges from X Factor, analysing everything we did. Thankfully, it didn't affect my second-year results. But it still demoralized me; I don't like to make errors. And when I received the outcome letter from the university, I feared the worst. My fellow students really helped me through a difficult year. I was also starting to lose interest in becoming a coach and working in the leisure industry. I was now looking to work in education or in healthcare with children because I wanted to help them on their educational journey and give them the support I never had.

I pushed myself to go to a Chelsea game with BD during the second year. This was a terrifying experience. BD was more passionate, outgoing and confident, and I don't think he understood how out of my comfort zone I was. From travelling there by bus and train, to the walk up to Stamford Bridge alongside more than 40,000 fans, some of whom were rowdy West Ham supporters, I was really pushing my limits. Before the game, he wanted to go to the pub with other raucous Chelsea fans, which I felt uncomfortable with. And I don't like to drink. I'm not great around drunkenness and social situations, so I just wanted to get to my seat and watch my team play.

I can't remember the result. I think I was on edge the whole time. This was exacerbated when we were leaving the ground. The fans were making their way home, there were many families among them, when suddenly, police on horses crossed our path as angry West Ham fans wielded bottles and flares. At that point, I was terrified. They were blocking the way to the train station and bus stop. But thankfully, it ended okay, and BD took care of me. It was terrifying though, and something I wasn't used to.

During my last year, the stress and depression really hit me. After seven years of higher education, I was struggling. Despite wanting to give up, I have always been someone determined to complete a task and was determined to finish my degree. I was no longer enjoying the educational side of university. But, as with everything in life, I continued to give 100 per cent in my studies. I was spending more time with my Uni family who were now living off campus. During that final year I decided to do something nice for each friend, so got them all a present and a card for their birthdays. For the first time in my life, I felt as if I fitted in somewhere and I wanted to show my appreciation. I used to love going on outings with SH; we used to share everything, and SH became one of my favourite people at university. Like the previous year, we attended many social events, including the end-of-year Summer Ball (2010 and 2011), which was a massive thing for me because it was an all day and night event. Activities included a live gig, silent disco - where you get headphones and choose what music to listen to while you dance along with everyone else listening to their music of choice - and The Bop among other things. DJ

Calvin Harris and English indie rock band The Pigeon Detectives performed, which was amazing. Comedian Russell Howard performed too, which was a good experience.

I reiterate at this point that were it not for my friends and lecturers, I don't think I would've reached the end. As we entered the final six months of university life, I had had enough and suffered another breakdown. Everything was becoming too much for me and I completely shut myself off from the world. I was missing lectures, neglecting my friends and was really behind with my assignments. So much so that I had six weeks to finish three assignments and my dissertation. I worked non-stop over the Easter holidays to catch up and it took so much out of me. The dissertation from hell was one of my biggest challenges. It was a notational analysis of five European and five African teams in the 2010 FIFA World Cup. In what was quite a poor tournament, I had recorded 30 matches on VHS to analyse and record the statistics. This became very dull and draining because I had to take down the number of shots, corners, throw ins and other stats for both teams in the game. It was all too much, and forever put me off academic writing and higher education. In general, the third year was overwhelming, and I was so relieved to get through it. Despite the difficulties I was so proud of my results and the pride on Mum and Nan's faces on graduation day was palpable.

AH, one of my favourite people, came to see me during the final year and invited me to a gig in Brixton where her then boyfriend's band was playing. I was terrified, but after a lot of persuasion I decided to go along. We took a cab and having had a previous experience in Brixton - a social event in secondary school - I was dreading the return. We left the event late and I was offered drugs on a few occasions and saw several shifty characters walking the streets. This time I had AH with me, so I felt a little more at ease. But what was great about her is how I felt she really understood me and how much it took for me to go to the event. Again, it was overwhelming: the loud noise and the big crowd around me. But I got through it. Like many things in my life, even when I am on edge and not wanting to be somewhere, I will try to do it for someone I care about. AH was proud of me and grateful I came with her.

That year was also my 21st birthday. I made it a themed party: heroes and villains. I went as The Mask of Zorro but left both my mask and toy sword at home. So really, I was just a guy in a cape! I invited people from all walks of life: family, friends from university, camp, college and secondary school, which was amazing. A number even came in costume: Captain America, Al Capone and The Riddler.

Arriving on time, I was anxious while waiting for others to arrive. I didn't really understand the term "fashionably late" at the time, so after about 30 minutes of waiting I was beginning to fear the worse - that nobody outside family was coming. In the end they did, and it was an amazing night, although I was again pressured into getting drunk. I particularly remember AM, BP, OS and DH coercing me to do a Flaming Sambuca, in which you drink a shot of the Italian liqueur after it has been lit. My attempt was being recorded on a phone. Drinking it involved licking salt, blowing out the flame on the drink, and downing it in one - which I did in the wrong order. It was an unforgettable night with some of my favourite people.

While in final year I had heard it was a popular thing to take a gap year post graduation. In another crazy moment, I applied for an internship through a company called SWEP to work as a hotel entertainer in Tenerife. This is one of the most out-of-my-comfort-zone things I have ever done, but once again I wanted to test myself. As my love for all things Spanish had grown over the years, I looked to make use of my language skills and spend six months in the sun. It turned out to be one of the best decisions I've ever made. An unforgettable 2011-2012 was about to unfold.

Graduation day with mum 2011

CHAPTER 8

MIS AVENTURAS EN TENERIFE — MY BIGGEST CHALLENGE TO DATE

AFTER an exhaustive seven years of higher education, I stepped out of my comfort zone again.

I was drained after a number of arduous years, but I wanted to test myself and figure out what I was truly capable of. What better way than to become a hotel entertainer in the Canary Islands. The process of getting there was a little more straightforward than with America but juggling university and everything else still made it a daunting prospect. It was actually more difficult once I was there because I had to obtain a Spanish bank account and fill out numerous forms.

September 2011 came around and it was again time for me to leave my family, which was always so difficult. Just as when I boarded the plane for America, I was really hesitant and nervous as I said my goodbyes to Mum. With a deep breath, I proceeded to boarding and I was on my way to Tenerife. There, I was greeted by the wonderful CL who had helped me greatly throughout the application process. She drove me to the hotel where I would be working for the next six months. During the drive, I saw how beautiful the island was. The mountain, El Teide stood tall and spectacular, and we were surrounded by the ocean. The culture was so different from home.

At the hotel, I met my boss, CB. He is one of the most confident, enthusiastic and supportive people I have ever met. I was still petrified but CL reassured me. CB gave me a tour of the hotel. At first glance, it looked like a labyrinth with numerous pathways and floors, but I soon realized it wasn't too bad. After a quick look around I was taken poolside, which is where the hotel's entertainment department was based. That first day I saw the staff perform the ABBA musical of Mamma Mia - and it wouldn't be the last time I saw that. While watching them rehearse, I was greeted by not only my hotel's staff, but also staff from another hotel down the road. Staff tended to rotate from hotel to hotel and also shared props and sets for the shows. I was introduced to my entertainment team. They were CB, AD, AG, SR, DR, SR, LH and CB from my hotel, and MS, DL and AW from the hotel down the road.

After watching the team rehearse and getting an early indicator of just how difficult this would be, I was taken up to my room. I am immensely grateful for the free food and accommodation; however, the staff quarters were really poor. But in hindsight, it didn't matter too much. We literally slept there, that's all. The rest of the day we were working - from 8am until around midnight. Thankfully in Spain they have a siesta period alongside a lunch hour, and honestly, due to my energy issues I don't think I would have made it to the end of my contract without that three-hour recovery period!

A typical day in the life of a hotel entertainer will show you how much effort they put in, and how hard they (and I) had to work. The day began at 8:00am. We would get together in the staff room and get given our jobs for the day. Most days we had to put away seating and tables from the previous evening. We might then have to set up the stage for the show, which meant changing the curtains and setting up props, and sometimes put out the exercise bikes for the spin classes. You rarely did the same thing two days running, which was great. At around 8:30am we would head off on our rounds of the poolside to promote forthcoming shows and events. There were so many choices at our hotel including French bowls, archery, beach football and volleyball, table tennis and so much more. We also had bingo, darts and bowling daily, with the winners given their prizes later in the evening. Then there were spin classes - as I mentioned - and aqua aerobics available for guests to keep in shape. After a few months, I let my boss know about my passion for working with children. I was then posted to the mini club working with four-to-eight-year-olds, making sure they had fun and letting their parents have some time to themselves.

After we'd gathered the guests who were up for some fun, the day was well under way. The initial activity lasted a couple of hours, until lunchtime, around 12:30pm. There were occasions where we had to rehearse for shows or set up specific activities, dependent on the numbers we had. Resuming an hour later, the afternoon was pretty similar to the morning session. Around 4:00pm was the siesta period where we had three hours to ourselves. For me it was an opportunity to sleep and recuperate. Six-plus hours in the heat of Tenerife takes a lot out of you.

After dinner we would come back, around 7:30pm, put on our *chalecos*, which is a shiny, colourful waistcoat, and began preparation for the evening shows. Our tasks varied again because some of us were performing, some were doing PR and some were working backstage on the technical side. Before the main event, you usually had the mini disco, which lasted about 30 minutes. I led the dancing and did this virtually every evening. I was absolutely terrified. I was performing in front of guests coming to see the main show and in front of lots of children who were mimicking the set dance routines of a number of songs that I was demonstrating. It was terrifying but something I am still proud of, that I pushed myself to do it.

After mini disco came the awards ceremony where the day's winners collected their prizes. At 9:00pm the main show kicked off. It usually incorporated hired professionals, such as circus acts or magicians, or a hilarious drag act put on by my friend SH who dressed up as Mister Sister. Two or three times a week we also performed in hilarious shows. My particular favourite was called Crazy Medley. This involved around 30 minutes of CB and AG switching costumes at ridiculous speeds, imitating famous personalities. They needed our help to change, which was incredibly stressful. One minute they would pop out as Freddie Mercury, the next they'd come out as Marilyn Monroe. Very entertaining but very exhausting. There was also a comedy sketch show featuring everyone, and on Sundays, on a two-week loop, we performed the musicals Mamma Mia and the Queen musical, We Will Rock You.

But the day wasn't over yet. We would then do our curtain call to all the cheers, before the end-of-the-day dance where we asked members of the audience to join us on stage. We'd then spend some time saying good night and thank you to the special guests, then did more PR. Communicating with strangers scares me. But after a few weeks I had a script rehearsed to ease the pressure on myself. But when the programme changed, and I had to learn it all anew, I really did struggle. There were even some evenings my anxiety was so bad that I sat in the toilet. But anyway, this gives you an idea of how hard these performers work each day.

Back to the early weeks of my time there, and I really did struggle to adjust and fit in. My first day off, I had a wander around my new surroundings. I walked a while along the beach and came across some people playing volleyball. Turned out it was an Olympic qualifying match ahead of London 2012. Tired from my walk, I entered the small arena to watch the match unfold. It was a beautiful place and somewhere I would definitely like to return to one day.

For the first week, unbeknown to me, I accidently ate in the main restaurant. I never realised until I was told staff had their own restaurant. The food, generally, was amazing in the hotel, as were the staff. I met AR and CB who were waitresses, and the legend that was JD who provided me with so many free drinks. I don't think I would've made it without them. Week two was when I think things got a little easier. I was introduced to new roommates, AO and Ulrich. AO was also from London. I finally had someone from the UK to share this experience with. After a week on my own, I wanted to try harder to make friends. The first person I became particularly close to was my partner in crime, DR. She really helped me get through the first few months before she had to leave and go back to the Netherlands. She introduced me to mini club, helped me learn the routines and supported me when I was really struggling. One evening, on our day off, we walked along the beach, wrote our names in the sand, had some nice food and ended up on a bench overlooking the ocean. I do believe we had feelings for each other at this point. However, typically in my case, she was to leave soon after. However, in that moment, we were just lying next to each other on the bench listening to the waves crash and just enjoying each other's company.

Most of my days off involved tedious activities. Doing laundry, going to the Mercadona (local supermarket) to buy food, learning routines and relaxing on the beach. Some nights I used to love sitting out there on my own, enjoying that feeling of serenity and peace one can get from watching and listening to the waves crash. It was an incredible sensation and I believe enhanced my ambition to one day move to a resort town with my family. On my days off, I also made a habit of going for a €3 breakfast at a local Gordon Ramsay restaurant. Absolutely loved it there. A great way to start the day.

As with everything in my life, I was giving it my all. But during the first month it became apparent that I was struggling to fit in. I found it tough to adapt to the rigorous schedule that being an entertainer threw at you, and the immense anxiety I had to deal with every day. I was determined to see it through, something which a number of other professionals were actually unable to do. Around Christmas time I went to an end-of-year-party with the staff. I will never forget what my boss CB, who was drunk at the time, said to me that evening.

"You know, in the early weeks you were not quite what I was looking for and I was close to letting you go. However, although you aren't the best entertainer, you are one of the most passionate, determined and hardworking people with the biggest heart, and I'm so glad I kept my patience as you have improved so much. I'm proud of you."

This truly touched me because I was spending my first Christmas and new year away from family and was really homesick. It gave me the drive to keep going and see out my six months. I was so privileged to have CB and the team around me. They were all so supportive and as time passed more accepting and understanding of me, despite not being the entertainer they had hoped to see. This in turn gave me some leeway, especially when performing in shows, because I was unable to do any of the big parts. I slowly grew into larger roles, but nothing compared to the others.

One of my first tasks was to sit in front of the restaurant as a statue playing a game of chess with AO. We weren't allowed to move a muscle no matter what the guests did. They kissed us, poked us, pulled our ears and noses, and tried everything to get us to break character. Like the chess board, we were dressed and painted entirely in black and white. A surreal couple of hours but funny, nonetheless. This was the first of many costumes I had to wear during my time at the hotel. The worst one by far was the company's mascot, Smiley the Dog. Just try to envisage putting on a dog costume in 30 plus degree heat and strutting around for hours. Again, we were not allowed to talk or break character, although the guests treated me better than when I was the chess-playing statue. Getting hugs from parents and children made the experience more enjoyable. After taking off the dog costume's head, buckets of sweat poured out. Exhausting, but rewarding and fun.

The entertainment sector can be a bit of a revolving door, as I've said before, so once one staff member leaves another has to come along and fill that role. IL, DB, LL, and SA replaced a number of leavers. SA was someone I took to straight away and alongside DR, MS, DL and JS, was someone I really started to like. I loved her positivity and drive. I was in awe of the talent, professionalism and hardworking mentality of everyone, of course.

I was, at this point, in charge of the mini club. SA came to join me so we could lead it together. I spent Christmas with her. A wonderful memory. We spent the day together going to restaurants, buying enormous drinks and having a pizza. But this was another occasion when I froze up. I wanted to tell her how I felt about her but for a large part of the meal, I was over-thinking everything, unable to say anything. She kept asking me if I was OK, but the mental block had well and truly jammed in place. I was afraid of rejection, afraid of the effect it would have on our friendship and just generally fearing the worst. After what felt like an eternity, I did say what I wanted to say and didn't get the answer I had hoped for. It was still an amazing evening though. We even saw Santa on a moped. He rode up to us, ringing his bell, and we had a photo with him. I'm still close to

SA to this day and I care about my Belgian buddy immensely.

Another girl I really took to was DL. A beautiful girl from Hungary. She worked in the nearby hotel. Typically, I waited an eternity to build up the courage to tell her how I felt. And in a rare moment in my life, my feelings were reciprocated. She gave me her number and we went on a date. In a cruel twist of fate, she was leaving the following day, which was devastating and so typical of my luck. I had a lovely evening with her. We spent the time talking about everything. At the end of the evening, in a rare burst of confidence, I even tried to kiss her! In hindsight, she was probably right to step back as she was going home the next day. We had a long hug as I was really sad to see her go, and we parted ways. Another friend, MS, never knew how I felt about her until recently where I told her on social media. She also worked at the other hotel and came to perform with us on occasion.

The final person I liked was actually one of the guests. I fell for JS quite early on and she is honestly one of the biggest hearted people you will come across. A couple of the entertainers and I went to speak to her and her wonderful family. We spent hours chatting about everything, the good and the bad. I think she realised quite early on that I was desperately out of my comfort zone. She was beautiful inside and out, and after the others went to bed, we stayed up talking. It's something I will never forget. A truly special family. I'm privileged they are a part of my life.

The entertainment team never failed to deliver on special occasions such as Halloween, Christmas and new year. The holiday periods were no doubt the busiest but were also a source of great memories. For Halloween, I dressed as Jigsaw, the serial killer from the movie Saw. This was a crazy day with all the make-up, and LL did an incredible job with it. It was melting in the heat as I rode a bike around the poolside and ran mini club, but it was really good fun. Christmas was a bit more cheerful because most of us were dressed as elves. We handed out presents to the children and everyone had fun. For New Year's Eve, tons of balloons had to be inflated. They were going to be secured in a net and would be released when the clock struck midnight. It felt like an eternity for us, blowing them all up. Being away from my family over the holidays was really difficult. However, by this point I had my Tenerife family to help me celebrate.

But from early on I felt I was struggling to fit in - apparent in the boundless energy shown by other members of the entertainments team. After finishing up most evenings, they would go out to places such as Las Veronicas, the night club district in Costa Adeje.

Although I managed to push myself once in a while and go with them, generally my tiredness, after giving everything during the day, caught up with me and I went to bed. Despite my struggles and my anxiety, I feel most people understood and accepted me, in spite of my differences.

To break the monotony of our weekly schedule, we took part in some team building days. Paintballing was a highlight, as was a boxing session. I had an opportunity to win at paintballing. Everyone else on my team had been eliminated in a capture-the-flag competition, so it was up to me to bring it home. I ran with everything I had towards where I believed the flag was hoisted. When I got there, I couldn't see it. And inevitably, I was shot. Had I pinpointed the flag, I had the pace to outrun the opposition and bring it back for the team. Nonetheless, both events were a welcome break and enjoyable occasions where the team bonded further.

Generally speaking, I was fearing the worst every single time I took to the stage or was centre stage during any activity. Having said that, I gave my all whether it was as a card dealer at casino night, the end-of-evening dance with the team, the minor roles I took on in Mamma Mia and We Will Rock You or the sketch shows (including performances as Robin Hood in The Men In Tights and The Backstreet Boys performing

Everybody), which was probably the most terrifying experience of my life. Every time I had to do the mini disco with so many eyes fixed on me, I was petrified. But I did my best. I did not want to let CB or my team down. Even when helping backstage on shows like Crazy Medley, or waiting to go on stage myself, the never-ending anxiety was at times too much. But still I got through it, and frankly, Tenerife is probably the closest I have come to reaching my potential and showing what I am truly capable of. I pushed above and beyond, and it's something I always look back on with great pride.

There were fun times. A prank some of them played on SR was amusing. I walked out of the hotel and saw my Italian friend's bicycle covered in duct tape.

While I was attending to my duties one day, in the craziest of coincidence, I heard somebody calling my name from a distance. Out of nowhere my friend MH and his partner appeared. This was one of my friends from Elliott School, and of all the places they could holiday, they chose the hotel I was working at! He had no idea I was there, but it was wonderful to see him again.

There were so many funny moments involving the staff and guests which added to the wonderful Tenerife adventure.

In December, Mum and her partner at the time, John, came to visit. It was the week of her birthday.

During their time in Tenerife, I still was working my usual days, but we did get to eat together. On my free days, we went on a trip to El Teide and Loro Parque, both of which were really nice excursions, and it was good to spend a bit of time away from the hotel.

On Mum's birthday we got her to come up on stage and got the crowd to sing happy birthday, rewarding her with one of the medals. It was a really nice moment. And Mum got to see me perform on stage, seeing a side of me she had never seen before. It was surreal for Mum to see this side of me, and she was really proud of the progress I had made. But she had to go home that same day, which resulted in me suffering a terrible bout of homesickness because it was the first Christmas, new year and birthday I had spent away from home.

It was really difficult saying goodbye to her, especially as a few weeks later SA also went home. I was feeling very homesick and wanted to end it there, however, I also wanted to get to the end of my contract, being the completist I am.

Towards the end of my time in Tenerife, it was my birthday. Although most of the day was business as usual, I did get a special mention in the evening where I was given a medal and love from the staff and audience, which was really nice. But little did I know this was just the beginning. When the evening ended, my friends converged on me and threw me into the ice-cold pool at around midnight. After getting changed, they took me to Las Veronicas, which was a really difficult environment for me because of the loud music, bright lights and large crowds. Not my scene at all. But I couldn't say no on my birthday. As with my 21st, there was a lot of peer pressure and drinking involved. I recall having around 14 shots during the course of the evening, before being put in a taxi home. I was so lightheaded as I made my way to my room, struggling to put the key in the lock before passing out on my bed without taking my clothes off. Thankfully, I had the following day off, so I had time to recover. But it was a great evening - up until I had too much to drink. To be fair, despite my usual difficulties and anxieties that come to the fore with outings like this, I did feel more at ease around people who truly cared for me.

Despite the fears that came with PR, I made some really lovely friends, particularly with some of the parents whose kids I took care of at mini club. The Thomsons, Lynches, Taskers, Bennetts and Chapmans are lovely families that I am still in touch with today.

Another one was the Waters family. They'd had too much to drink one evening. I was doing PR, and out of nowhere I was put into a crazy position where one of the women from the family wanted to kiss me. I froze, as I always do in those situations; I felt so uncomfortable. She gave me a really long smooch. There was nothing I could do. Funny looking back. Another family that deserves a special mention are the Slusarczyks, who are some of the most wonderful people I had the pleasure of meeting.

Saying goodbye to SA in January really summed up a difficult, few weeks at the hotel. Not wanting to be alone in mini club again, I was desperate for her to stay. Although she had second thoughts, she had to go, sadly. We embraced, said we loved each other and parted ways, which was really difficult. As she was heading to the airport, I messaged her asking her to come back. She, for a moment, gave me false hope by saying she was going to return. But it wasn't to be. By this point I had made several wonderful friends including MB, CD, KV, JU, GB, as well as my wonderful colleagues from both hotels. So as sad as I was, I still had several wonderful people to get me through the final two months.

As you can tell by the way I have written about my time in Tenerife, it truly was the best time of my life, and I am forever grateful to everyone who got me through to the end. I am appreciative of the patience shown by CB and his understanding of my specific circumstances. Everyone I met there will always have a place in my heart. On a personal note, I was so proud of all I achieved, especially considering the previous seven years of higher education and all that had happened prior to this adventure. Saying goodbye to everyone was really difficult. But I was ready to go home. I feel I achieved everything I could from working abroad. As I headed home, I really wasn't prepared for what was in store and had an immediate reality check on arrival at Gatwick airport.

Above: Performing the end-of-show dance with the rest of the entertainment staff.

Below: With the work family on my final evening in Tenerife.

Above: Halloween at the hotel with AJ.

Below: Sandra and me spending Christmas eve in Costa Adeje and coming across Santa on a moped.

Above: Christmas in Las Dalias, really hectic day.

Below: Daisy and me performing as Lolly and Pop for the children.

CHAPTER 9

THE RETURN TO A "NEW WORLD" AND A FALSE DIAGNOSIS

WHEN I returned to the UK, my mum and sister greeted me at the airport. Fresh from Spain, with a new level of confidence and being accustomed to the Spanish culture, I kissed them each on the cheek, which was so unlike me. I had done it so much in Tenerife with guests that it had become second nature.

It was safe to say I was mentally and physically exhausted after an arduous, few years. This was the start of what was to be a very difficult time personally, which began with a significant new adjustment. While in Tenerife, my family had left London, after many years of discussion, and settled in Surrey. After all we had been through, growing up in South-West London, Mum decided for the good of the family that it was time to move on. Sadly, we had to leave a lot of family and friends behind, and unfortunately my nan and uncles did not take it very well.

I came home exhausted but probably the most upbeat I'd been in a long time and was ready and willing to push forward with my life. But adjusting to things in Epsom and Ewell was really difficult. I was unaware at how much tension there was within the family until I pushed myself to go and visit the Roehampton branch of the family. Honestly, I felt like a stranger entering the house. A place I once called my second home, filled with some of the most special people in my life, became incredibly uncomfortable - which was an awful feeling. I remember entering the house to awkward glances. I genuinely had no idea what had happened. Granddad was happy to see me, Nan was sketchy, but the kicker was when I saw my uncles come in from the back garden and upon seeing me, they hesitated to come over and greet me. That was the moment I realised just how badly they'd taken to Mum moving away. I was broken up to see what had happened while I was away. It was the beginning of what was to be several losses and divisions among friends and family in the following years. Distraught, I returned home, and Mum explained what had happened in my absence.

It was 2012, and like all my siblings, Isabelle had become a victim of bullying. Something we've all had to deal with in our lives, sadly. Summer was now 18 and making great strides in her life. She aspired to be a policewoman and was really committed to her studies. She had also begun working as a hotel worker at Chessington World of Adventures. Tee-Jay was really struggling to adjust to life in Surrey, especially as he was in the process of undertaking his IT degree at Roehampton University. Thankfully, he had a great deal of support, and the university were incredibly accommodating. They provided a cab to take him to and from his classes and he would be greeted by someone on arrival at campus who would take him to his class. He also had a support worker who took notes on his behalf and aided him on his educational journey.

Mum made the decision to move for the betterment of her children, and to this day we all feel it was the right decision. Despite having all my family and friends in London I'd had so many negative experiences there. It was a difficult transition, but I knew it was the right call to get out of there. It was around early 2012 when we also decided to get some new pets. We got a tiny puppy who we called Henry first, and then a few months later we got another one who we named Poppy. They were a much-needed addition as my brother and I have always got on better with animals than humans, and with the recent loss of loved ones, we were happy to welcome these dogs into our home.

While I'd been in Tenerife, Mum had been sending out CVs for me to try to find me a job for when I came home. Within a few weeks of settling into life in Epsom, I already had an interview for a job at a nursery. Everything was moving so fast. But ever willing to make my family proud, and with the high standards I set myself, I went along and got a trial placement at Cherryfield.

Despite knowing from day one that the age range wasn't the one I wanted to work with, I gave it my all for two-to-three months. I was in a mostly female environment and being the only male was a tough adjustment. I did meet some lovely people whilst there including LB, KW, LC, JP and SP; however, I once again struggled to fit in - a familiar theme throughout my life. Cycling to and from work and giving my all three times a week was draining. I remember sleeping during the lunch hour on a number of occasions due to sheer exhaustion! During my time there, I developed feelings for JP and SP, which I feel was almost inevitable due to the environment. But as was often the case in my life, the feelings weren't mutual. With all that was happening around me, I was really starting to struggle again, and, after leaving the nursery, I felt the last decade finally catch up with me. Years and years of suppression finally came to a head and I had another breakdown.

With all that had occurred in my life thus far, this is where I began researching what could be wrong with me. I had to know. With the knowledge of my brother's condition, I was beginning to think that I may have similar difficulties. Despite where I was mentally, I continued to be there for my brother. We joined a golf club, which I feel we both needed at the time. We had many enjoyable days on the golf course, and it was a welcome distraction from everything going on around us. We joined the gym, took the dogs out, and did anything to keep our minds occupied. I was determined to not let my mental health get the better of me, but the constant loss and estrangement of family and friends took its toll, and I began to feel truly isolated. I went to see the doctor in late 2012 hoping for a formal diagnosis. I had to undergo a number of tests and was labelled as having Asperger syndrome. I already knew I had generalised anxiety disorder and clinical depression, but this new diagnosis was confirmed following the consultation. I felt like a huge weight had been lifted off my shoulders and that I finally had some answers going forward in life. Little did I know however, until a few years ago, that this was not an official diagnosis, although I was under the impression that it was at the time.

In 2012, I also suffered a big family loss with the death of Granddad David. I have always struggled with watching others suffer, or hearing about them passing away on the news, but when it happened to me personally, it really affected me. I didn't think I could attend the funeral alone, so my mum came with me, despite the daunting prospect of coming face to face with my dad and his new wife. This, I believe, was the last time I saw my dad, my half-siblings and most of my family on his side in person, which is devastating. I do still try to see Aunty Sarah when possible, but aside from that I sadly haven't seen any of them since moving here. It was a lovely service though and wonderful to see my family; but it was clouded by awkwardness and tension, which made it an even more difficult occasion.

After a difficult six months or so coming to grips with everything, Mum got me a driving lesson for my birthday in early 2013. Having had a phobia of driving for a long time, this was another challenge for my progression.

I have been afraid of driving for as long as I can remember. I was nearly run over by a truck back in my school days, so it goes back to that incident I believe. However, there are other factors involved too. I just really don't like the responsibility of being behind the wheel of a large metal machine. One mistake and your life could be over, or you could seriously hurt someone else, which is a serious put-off for me. The costs of owning and maintaining a car are also astronomical and I've always felt my spatial awareness isn't great, so being behind the wheel has always felt a daunting task.

But on my birthday, I had my first and only driving lesson. It was a terrifying experience, but I gave it a go. The driver took me on some quiet roads and gave me instructions on how to drive. It started okay because I was driving on a straight bit of road at a decent speed. However, after struggling with a turn, I had the realisation of what I was doing. Going down another straight, I had an anxiety attack and, to the instructor's astonishment, froze, almost crashing into a nearby car. The instructor, luckily, took the controls and stopped us in time.

As I'd thought, my spatial awareness isn't great, so I decided to end the lesson there, having been put off driving for a long time. I was still okay with go-karts and smaller vehicles but when behind a wheel it was too much for me to handle. I was proud that I had given it a go, but I was happy to continue to use my bicycle and public transport when I had to.

I had been, in recent months, looking for another job that wasn't as intensive as my previous ones had been. I had come across a nearby place in Chessington that worked with special needs children called the Moor Lane Centre. After another nerve-racking interview and training process, I made them aware of my specific needs and difficulties. Instead of being given a full-time placement I ended up working in a Saturday club, six hours a week, with some wonderful staff and kids. We did all sorts - taking them to London Zoo, London Aquarium, local farms and special centres, as well as on occasion staying at Moor Lane, which had everything you needed for a fun day.

I really struggled adjusting to the severe needs of some of the young adults and after a few sessions my anxiety surrounding toileting and changing them, for example, became too much. I had wonderful colleagues though and from then on, I took care of the less severe individuals. One person in particular, named Guy, really helped me settle in and showed me the ropes, getting me through some very difficult first few months. It was a thoroughly rewarding experience in which I stayed for two years.

My weekly routine was beginning to come together nicely. I was being a great carer to my brother, had a stable, not too overwhelming job, and was enjoying time to myself. Things were starting to improve once more. Forever trying to gain a better understanding of myself, I turned to social media in the hope of finding like-minded people. I have met some of the best people online and some have kept me going when I lost complete faith in myself. Isn't it crazy how people you have never met can be at times more influential, accepting and understanding than people who have been friends for years? Having said that, I was always willing to keep in touch with people from my past and I still tried to push myself to see friends from university and college. Wandsworth football was still going strong, and I tried on occasion to go on public transport to see them. Football was always a great escape and the chance to catch up with some of the better people in my life was always a pleasure. It is funny, though, that despite them being some of my favourite people I still struggled to fit in. When having breaks during football, I either sat on my own or with the others but being quiet, just listening and finding out how they were progressing in their lives.

In a year that started so well, it quickly turned into the worst year of my life. I suffered some big losses, which changed my life forever. At a time when I needed loved ones more than ever, I was unable to open up and ask for support. So, like much of my life to this point, I dealt with everything on my own. In the end everything came crashing around me in what was a moment I will never forget.

CHAPTER 10

THE FINAL STRAW - TY AND THE DAY THAT CHANGED EVERYTHING

I HAVE always struggled around death. I have this weird superstition: every time I have a negative thought about myself or a loved one, I knock on wood as it is the last thing I want. I don't honestly know how I would react to another significant loss. I really struggle nowadays to watch the news as most things reported are negative, and it tears me up inside to see what a cruel world we live in.

As I've already said, this had started off being a really positive year. But it was all about to change. One day, I'd gone to work at the Moor Lane Centre as normal. My expectations of an ordinary day were shattered however, when I was told that one of my good friends there had passed away. I was shocked and upset. Guy was someone who had really helped me settle in at the centre, and I had no idea he was terminally ill. To have been in his condition and still work with special needs children, I think, is so admirable. He was a wonderful man with a big heart. Naturally, I mourned and tried to keep going to make him and the others around me proud - which leads me to the worst day of my life.

Two days after I heard of Guy's death, I received a call early in the morning from the Netherlands; I recognised the Dutch number. Normally I don't answer unknown numbers, but I figured it was my dear friend Ty who I had stayed in contact with since our devastating parting of the ways at Camp America.

I answered. It was her boyfriend. He told me that the once love-of-my-life had taken her own life. She had overdosed, and one of the most beautiful, genuine and wonderful people I ever met was no longer with us.

I haven't been the same since that phone call.

He asked if I wanted to attend the funeral, but I said I was too anxious to go to the Netherlands. Tears streamed down my face. My brother, who had just woken up, overheard the conversation. But again, unable to open up or seek support, I suppressed my hurt and dealt with it all alone.

I will never forget April 2013 and even now I really struggle during that month as it reminds me of the worst week of my life.

I shut myself off from the world. Aside from work, I could barely do anything for months. Distraught and desperate for help I went to see the GP and explained everything that had happened. The doctor prescribed medication to alleviate my depression. She also gave me contact details for local charities, clubs and courses. With the information provided I looked online and come across specific work and social opportunities in the Epsom area. After a few months, starting from rock bottom, I began finding my way back to where I want to be. I kept myself distracted by doing activities with my brother and sister. Tee-Jay, Izzie and I regularly went out on dog walks, bike rides and played sports in the multi-sports centre, the field and the tennis courts situated near our house. Summer, by that time eighteen, was really starting to get her life in order and worked long hours at the Chessington World of Adventures Resort, so we mostly interacted after she came home from her job. Tee-Jay and I also joined a gym. Initially my brother's idea, this again turned out to be a much-needed distraction and another opportunity for us both to get out and about. I used to love going swimming and I do still miss that.

Back at home, things were getting more difficult for my brother and me. Our dog Henry had grown increasingly aggressive, making it impossible to move around our house without him attacking us. He had gone for all of us at some point. It got so bad my brother couldn't leave his bedroom, so I had to force myself to get things for him. Entering the living room hesitantly, Henry would glare at me and bare his teeth. It was a difficult situation for all of us and because we loved him, we were patient with him for a long time. But after almost a year, and no signs of improvement, we were sadly forced to give Henry away. I was devastated but it wasn't right for us all to be so afraid walking around our own home.

It was getting difficult enough sharing a bedroom with my brother, especially during that distressing year, but we were also having to deal with extreme temperatures in our attic room. Really hot in summer, freezing cold in winter. I suffered many sleepless nights, not helped by the fact that my brother had his PC on until the early hours. The light from the computer beamed at my face and loud typing made it more difficult to get some sleep. It got so bad I had to buy a sliding door to separate the two halves of our room to cut out the light from the computer. Having all this going on really didn't help my state of mind.

So, I turned once again to social media for support and encouragement because I really was close to breaking point again. Honestly, online friends did more for me during this time than even some of my closest friends. I will be forever grateful to people like JY, LH and JP among many others, who have always supported me and been on my side.

I tried joining some more groups and pages, not only to tell my story but to raise awareness and show that even in the darkest times we can always find a way back into the light. The last words Ty said to me were, "I am always proud of you", and that is something I have taken on board. I want to continue to make family, friends and those I have lost proud. It is a great incentive to get back to where I aspire to be.

Around the middle of the year, I came across a local garden centre through the Richmond Fellowship, a mental health charity. The Old Moat Garden Centre was a wonderful place full of lovely people and for two years I went there once a week to volunteer and undertake numerous roles, such as watering the plants, weeding and working in the potting shed. This gave me an escape from all that was going on and was really therapeutic. I met a lot of great people there, none more so than SH who I developed strong feelings for while working there. At this point I was more suppressive than ever and, following previous experiences, I struggled to even talk to anyone about this, so it wasn't until much later that I told her how I felt. The bad luck struck again however as she was in a relationship, so I felt I had wasted a long time suppressing my feelings. If I'd asked right away, I would have known and wouldn't have been as upset with her revelation. I still care about this girl a lot and knowing all she has dealt with I value our friendship.

We were asked to be Christmas tree salesmen that December. This was a new and terrifying experience for me, but SH made the experience a lot more bearable, and at times fun. I also recall in the latter stages of my two-year stint regaining some confidence and working in the shop behind the cash register. Similarly, it was a daunting but positive experience. The customers were always friendly and frankly the Old Moat generally had a positive atmosphere. The summer months were really exhausting in the greenhouses with the sun beating down, but it really was a nice stress reliever from all that was going on elsewhere.

At this point, in the summer of 2013, I was slowly getting back on track. I was being a better carer for my brother, working twice a week at both Moor Lane

Centre and Old Moat Garden Centre and I feeling like I was on the road to recovery.

Although social media and being able to talk with likeminded people helped, it was also a source for negativity, and news I was trying to avoid. During this time a number of celebrity deaths upset me, but the one that shocked me the most was Robin Williams' passing. Not only was he a legend in the industry, movies like Flubber, Aladdin, Mrs Doubtfire and Jumanji were a big part of my childhood. Hearing how he died really did send shockwaves through me. He was a comedian who brought joy to the world yet behind closed doors he was a tortured soul fighting battles of his own. He had so much more to give but this world can be a cruel place and for some, it becomes too much. Another more recent loss was the lead singer of the band Linkin Park, Chester Bennington. I feel a status I posted on Facebook following his suicide summed up my thoughts very well:

> You know what upsets me most about this. People know it is a result of mental health and a lack of love, support and even a feeling of emptiness. What gets me is people will mourn and be upset (personally I didn't know his name but grew up enjoying Linkin Park and am gutted in this guy passing in his early 40s) but in a few days people will show the same ignorance and the stigma will continue. People don't listen, they don't actually

> stick by their loved ones. People with mental health issues are appreciative of the smallest gestures but people can be so self-centred they don't help until it is too late. People fight so much every day and speaking from personal experience hardly anyone is there for you really. You have to in large part fight alone, initiate or make the effort maintaining relationships or you become more isolated and alone and a spiral of depression occurs. I think there are less than a handful of friends and family who make an active effort in any way and some people reach that tipping point of having a breakdown, shutting off completely and in particular cases turning to vices or worse. They fight the battle alone every day and one day it overwhelms to the point of no return. Depression and anxiety are some of the worst things one has to deal with yet when one hears you are suffering; they turn the other way. Then you wonder why people like Chester turn to what they do. Seriously people show more love and empathy towards your friends and family as you may be the only one that does. We have one life so treat others how you expect to be treated and be there for those in difficult times. I have felt the agony of losing one of my best friends in a tragic way and I don't want anyone else to go through that. Love you all and I am always a message away, just wish it was more reciprocal RIP Chester.

During this torrid time, I once again found solace in TV, particularly US dramas and quiz shows. I also discovered a passion for the American wrestling promotion, Impact Wrestling, which I have watched almost every week since 2013. These things gave me an escape, and shows such as Fringe and Sons of Anarchy, among many others, helped me get through some difficult evenings. Another one I personally love, even now, is the US version of Whose Line Is It Anyway? I have always been a massive fan of Wayne Brady, Colin Mochrie and Ryan Stiles. Their improvisation and general talents never cease to cheer me up and entertain me, providing that escape. TV generally gave my brother and I another activity that kept us busy. Over the years, I had collected lot of box sets and DVDs, so I had plenty to keep my mind occupied.

In the summer of 2013, I decided to give online dating a try. These sites can be immensely demoralising and for people with conditions such as mine, it can be very hard to find a match, let alone find someone who understands the difficulties I have with communication and social interaction. Even signing-up to these apps is a challenge. Catfishing can be a problem - where someone creates a false profile to defraud people, financially or emotionally. People can just ignore you completely or initially take an interest before disappearing completely. After a few months of mostly little happening (although I did make a few friends through it), I met AC. We clicked right away and for months were messaging each other regularly. But I had also met HP on the site and started liking her. So, I faced a dilemma. It was a tough decision. But due to my anxiety around travelling, I chose AC because she lived in closer proximity.

Heading towards 2014, and wanting to try push myself again, we had a video call and arranged a date. Starting the year with renewed motivation and belief, we had our first date in Sutton. She was a single mum to the wonderful (then) two-year-old EC, so I was thrust into an unfamiliar environment. AC also had certain conditions, which eventually made our relationship impossible. I am going to try being as respectful as possible to her and her family as I take you through our six months together.

Our first date was a lovely outing, mostly walking around Sutton, getting to know one another. I opened up about my conditions, telling her everything I've told you in this book. She told me a lot about herself too, her past, her conditions, and her family. She'd had some really tough times. We said goodbye by having our first kiss. I remember that feeling of, "finally" in terms of having my first girlfriend and this overriding feeling of happiness for the first time since the traumatic loss of Ty.

We had a number of dates. We visited the Sea Life London Aquarium, took a lovely walk down by the

Thames, and went to the Tate. We also had an outing to Nonsuch Park in Epsom and Ewell, and then Worcester Park in Sutton. I think this was when we fell for each other. We were in a cafe and we held hands across the table. The first month or so was amazing but sadly it didn't last. It started to go downhill when we went to visit her parents. This was to become a recurring theme over the next five months. I had to push myself every week to get the bus and train to Sutton.

Although not totally innocent herself, AC's parents played a big part in our struggles. During our six-month relationship, her mother constantly spoke about me behind my back and tried to get her to break up with me. Honestly, her mum was like a modern-day Miss Havisham in Dickens' Great Expectations; she was determined to break my heart. I felt for AC. She had grown up with a father who had anger issues and a mother who was an alcoholic. One evening we were watching a UEFA Champions League match and having pizza. As usual, the table was cluttered with wine glasses. Her mum, MC, had drunk too much. PC, her dad, although he had a temper, was actually quite good to me. That evening, though, her mum lost it. There was screaming and arguing, which caused me to breakdown and cry. AC and her dad saw what it was doing to me and told the mother to leave. Honestly, it was a night I wanted to forget. But it exposed to me how much AC had suffered. It also exposed how alcohol addiction can drastically affect a person.

It wasn't until we'd broken up and my mum and sister revealed it to me, that I understood how much more I had put into our relationship than AC had. She'd visited my home only three or four times; I was at hers almost every week. They also thought I was being used financially. I gave absolutely everything to being the best boyfriend and "dad" to EC, but felt it was thrown in my face.

EC got really sick once and had to go to the hospital. I had a throat problem, pharyngitis, and AC's parents blamed me for their granddaughter's illness. I was devastated but it transpired that I wasn't to blame. She'd gone to hospital because of smoke inhalation.

I really struggled from that moment on, but I decided to stick by AC; I understood her conditions and past difficulties. After a number of break up attempts by AC I made one last effort by booking a Haven trip to Hastings. It was mostly a nice break, but I was starting to see similarities between AC and her mum. When she bought a bottle of wine from the shop, I began to fear the worst. However, because we were in Hastings, I thought it would be a lovely opportunity to catch up with the Morgans as they lived there. We took a long walk to the beach front and caught up with Mark,

Nathan and Nicole. Later in the day we also got to see Paula, who worked in a restaurant, and we had a lovely meal. On the whole it was a nice getaway, but it was marred by some negative moments.

I really loved her daughter and got to share in some big moments, such as her first day at nursery. I also witnessed her joy when she played on the slide and swings at the park. It was difficult, what with the early mornings and watching Disney Junior, but I did it all for them. We had some really lovely times, but the final straw was when I found out AC had cheated on me. Not only did she kiss her best friend, but when we were supposedly on a break, she'd got with another guy. These two betrayals broke me.

As much as I loved her and wanted to be with her, I had to let her go for the good of my health. In 2014, I had started attending the Brickfield Centre, for those who struggle with mental health issues. One day I'd gone there to have some time to myself and play pool with other members, when I received a call from AC. It was as difficult a conversation as the one I had with Ty's boyfriend. It began with another attempt to break up with me and I broke down. Realising she wasn't going to change because of her mother, I painfully agreed. But she had a sudden change of heart; realised the error of her ways and didn't want to end it after all! But after everything I had dealt with, as hard as it was, I stuck to my guns and decided to call it a day. It destroyed me. I truly adored her, despite all the issues. For me, it almost felt like a double break up - I lost her and her daughter, which was a lot to take. After losing EC I have since hoped one day to have a daughter of my own. The question I always ask myself, though, is how can one who struggles to take care of himself be responsible for another?

In the following weeks, there came a barrage of calls and texts which made me feel worse than ever. But at that point I just couldn't put myself through it anymore. Through consultation with my family, I blocked AC off completely, which is something I never want to do to anyone. A few years later I did unblock her to see how she was and now, although we are on OK terms, I am still terrified to go back to Sutton in fear of seeing her parents. It is safe to say AC was the best and worst thing to happen to me. But I will always care for her and EC, and they will always have a place in my heart.

Rest in Peace, Athaya (Ty). She is on my left in this photo.

CHAPTER 11

THE ROAD TO RECOVERY AND THE MOVE TO EASTDEAN

HAVING hit rock bottom again, I had to find my way back on my own. I did what I knew best and continued to keep myself busy - played sport and walked the dog with my brother, watched TV and hit the games console. Tee-Jay was really starting to improve his tennis and could keep rallies going at a good level. Having called it a day at Moor Lane, I now only had the garden centre as my escape. With everything I had gone through, this was so vital to my recovery, and I met a lot of lovely people there.

Because I didn't have a paid job, and not understanding my state of mind, my mum employed tough love, encouraging me to find work. Once we were at Homebase. She told me to give them my CV. But I just wasn't ready. It happened often when we were out and about, shopping, day's out. I finally gave up and started handing them out.

I didn't have much success finding anything or getting interviews in the careers I was interested in, so I decided to visit the Job Centre. This felt like a low point for me because I never wanted to be in this position.

Each week I went there was difficult. My anxiety was through the roof. And I had to cycle there in the early hours. I was afraid of going into that building every time with my "to-do" list of things I was expected to have done, and I was terrified I might lose my benefits if I failed to follow every step, every demand they made.

My increasing fear of public transport and travelling resulted in me only looking for jobs locally. And this went on for months until one day I began to open up to the work coach at the benefits' office and tell her about my conditions. And her response was positive.

There was a specialist work coach that helped people like me, and I transferred over to her. Through my interactions with her, I became aware of local charities and organisations, some which I had already used. But I was also introduced to the Hub Epsom, Work Stress Solutions and Aspire Supported

Volunteering among others, which help people with mental and physical difficulties.

After visiting the organisations, I decided to give education another go so looked at local courses - which led to a new ambition in life. To combine my love of children with education, and supporting those in need, it seemed logical to become a teaching assistant or learning support assistant. I applied for courses and started in 2015.

Before all this, though, I did suffer another tragedy. One of my former campers took his own life. The second time in three years I had to deal with a loss like this. I was devastated. It brought back memories of the good times and bad times in America, especially how it ended with Ty.

Just to compound my misery, we also lost Uncle Ron, a wonderful family member. Death as a theme was becoming all too familiar in the 2010s, and each loss hit me hard. Then Nanny Yvonne died too. Losing her and Uncle Ron was hard. She was a massive part of our childhoods. Although not related to me, she will always be my Nan and family to me, as will all the Wells. As I mentioned before, any sad news or death hurts me, and these bereavements came as a shock.

So as 2014 came to an end, I found myself once again turning to social media for support, finding others in a similar position. But this made things worse as I connected with many who were very close to giving up. Others like JY, SF, MH, and HR were there for me like I was there for them; we supported each other. More than anyone, HR was in a dark place. One night she spoke about self-harm and ending her pain. I was terrified and contacted a local Facebook group for advice. After hours, I talked her out of it, and I was so relieved; but that was a difficult evening.

As wonderful as it is to have likeminded people to talk to, you also have to handle them on their worst days, which can be overwhelming. This is when they need you the most. So if you're in that position, let them know they are loved and that they have so much more to give the world.

I went into 2015 with a similar attitude to the one with which I entered 2014: to find myself once more and do things out of my comfort zone and try to be like others around me.

I began the year by seeking to make friends locally. I used an app called Meetup. Aside from one group named the Epsom Rotaract, the others were tailored to the older generation, so I had to search further afield. This involved public transport again. But I did come across a Wimbledon Meetup group. They had Wombles in their name, obviously.

Before pushing myself too much, I thought it best to communicate with a few of the members online to get an idea of the environment, numbers, and activities, as well as letting them know how big a step this was for me.

After a few weeks I once again took a leap of faith and met CL from the group at Wimbledon station. We went to a bar they regularly went to, but when we walked in I was overwhelmed by how many people were there. I struggled to fit in, but I stuck with CL as she knew how hard it was for me. I spoke to a few people there and some of them made it bearable. The likes of SC, MW and CH. I attended a few of these evenings at different venues and remember one where we watched Six Nations rugby. As lovely as most of them were, I was again unable to socialise and integrate with the group, which is when I stopped going and started looking elsewhere.

I tried a Kingston Meetup at one point, which again was a really nice evening, held at the Rotunda where we bowled. Just three other people, which helped me. Sadly though, those people disappeared after that evening, so I had to try again to find a new group of friends.

That's when I came across Epsom Rotaract. I remember the first time I met this wonderful group of people was at The Faraday in Epsom where they were holding a *Friends* quiz. I thought that was the perfect event to attend and an opportunity to push myself. I was still nervous, so I brought Summer along and we both had a really nice time.

I also met HW that night. She became one of the best friends I have ever had. Unlike so many in my life, she has stuck by me. I really don't know what I'd do without her. I started liking her early on until I attended a Christmas dinner with the Rotaract and discovered she was seeing someone.

I was sad that evening, but it was a lovely event and I felt surprisingly at ease. Everybody was so accepting, and I have made some good friends through the group. A few months after we'd met, HW and I went to a local park. She had left her partner and I started to develop feelings for her again. We sat in the park, and I opened up to her about everything, something I'd not done with someone in a long while. HW opened up in similar fashion. It was the day I knew HW and I would be friends for life. Although in recent times I have become more isolated and distant from those outside my family, I know she will always be there, and she'll never give up on me.

Summer had also started seeing someone. He was called Elliott Blagrove, now my nephew's dad. As with any new presence in our home, it took my brother a while to adjust to him. Little do people know that I too am very similar with new people - and on occasion even with family. I let my anxiety get the better of me - so it took me months to introduce myself.

As the years have passed, Elliott has become family to me and another of my best friends. During the first year of our friendship, when I wanted to push myself and attend Wandsworth Park football, Elliott wanted to come along. He offered to drive. It was a really nice summer day. I got in his car; the roof was down. I felt good that day. I was starting to slowly find myself again.

Earlier in the year I had attended Cognitive Behavioural Therapy (CBT) lessons - after a long wait. Having struggled a lot the previous year, I'd again sought professional support through my GP. CBT was an interesting experience. I am not a great communicator, so saying what I've said in this book was hard to say to a therapist. Although not a big fan of talking therapy, I liked interacting, and even brought my mum to a session to give her more of an insight into what I'd been through.

It is refreshing to talk to someone who genuinely cares, listens, and doesn't judge you. It may have only been six sessions, but it did help me get back to a place where I could try again. But what made these sessions difficult is that around halfway through, I discovered that my

Granddad Colin had died. The closest person I have had to a father figure was no longer with us. To make matters worse, the family were still in conflict because of our move to Surrey, so I never really got to see him in his later years, which really did break my heart.

I hugged my therapist in one session soon after learning of his passing, because I just needed that affection and couldn't ask it of loved ones. I was so emotional. But with therapy, I feel that once it is all out there, it isn't until you leave the building that the emotions really hit you.

Granddad Colin's funeral was hard and full of awkwardness. Death again. I just find it so tough. But this time my brother - who wasn't used to this - and my family were there, making it doubly hard.

One moment destroyed me. As we entered the funeral parlour, my brother saw Granddad's coffin passing by in the hearse. He lashed out; he was so upset.

We said our goodbyes and then mixed as a family. It almost felt as if we had not spent the previous 20 odd years together as a close-knit family, and again I couldn't handle it. I am happy to say we are on better terms now but at this point it all just felt so different. It was awful. One to forget. Although Granddad Colin, like all those I have lost, is always in my thoughts.

Back at home things weren't much better. Mum's partner had become increasingly addicted to drink, which brought back memories of AC's mother. He'd had a stroke, and this was key to the change we saw in him, because in the earlier years, he'd been so great to be around. The downward spiral was evident. He continued to take advantage of Mum, often going to a bar and asking her to pick him up.

Inevitably it all came to a head. Summer had enough of how he was treating our mum and intervened. I couldn't; I just hate confrontation. But Summer was always more outspoken and capable, and she told Mum to leave him.

There was an evening of screaming. My brother got involved but I sat on the staircase struggling to cope. After years together, something had to change; it had become hopeless for them.

So, he left. It was sad. He'd been a big part of our lives for almost a decade. But somewhere along the line he'd lost his way. Mum was patient and had tried so hard to get him help. But he never took it.

I was still regularly attending the Brickfields centre. It was a great escape from everything, I was surrounded by likeminded people and the activities kept me busy. The professionals also helped me and kept me on track. And this is where I come full circle. One of the first things I mentioned in this book: the creative writing course. I also gave photography, arts and crafts and gardening a try. These were all necessary distractions during a difficult, few years.

I was starting to think about taking another leap of faith, too. Maybe a return to French Woods. I was also looking at other opportunities the internet had to offer. I filled out applications, pushing myself to call the respective companies. One thing that devastated me, and was a massive setback, was that a certain company wouldn't let me work with them because of some of my responses in my application with regards to mental health restrictions. I didn't let it deter me though. I looked up holiday rep organisations, including In2action and Powder Byrne, and pondered America again, perhaps as a member of staff at Disneyworld. Although some people accepted my application, I just wasn't ready to take the plunge, though.

Determined to keep trying and pushing myself, I continued with my pursuit of a potential career in education, which led me to undertake two separate courses in the hope of making it a reality.

I went to an open evening at Nescot College, in Ewell, and saw a Level 2 course in Principles of Working with People with Learning Disabilities. This was a distance learning course so I didn't have to worry about not fitting in and being anxious in the classroom; I could study at home.

Separately, I also began two Workers' Educational Association (WEA) courses in Epsom, a Level 1 course entitled Preparing to Help in Schools and a Level 2 coursc, Support Work in Schools. Returning to studies was a challenge. I had developed a distaste for it after my final year of university. However, I once again rose to the challenge and passed all the courses.

Furthermore, in what was another fulfilling moment for me, through my hard work on the Level 2 courses, I was awarded a certificate of achievement by the Festival of Learning - the biggest celebration of lifelong learning in England - which made me very proud.

Part of the Support Work in Schools course led me to my next voluntary work role, working at the wonderful Wallace Fields Infant School & Nursery (WFIS). Part of the course was practical and involved finding a school and taking weekly journal entries of the tasks undertaken and what we had learned. After completing my hours, I decided to stay on for another full school year after the summer holidays. The bike ride to and from that school was difficult though, and in the end made it impossible for me to continue. But for the first time in my life - not counting my times abroad - I genuinely enjoyed my job and wanted to stay.

WFIS was an amazing school with incredible kids and staff. I felt like one of the team from the off. Having said that, similar to my experience at Cherryfield Nursery, I was, aside from the janitor, the only man working there. At times that was difficult, particularly at lunchtimes. Once again, I was the quiet one. I was there once a week and was placed in the first term with Mrs L and the Year 2s. In the new year I got placed with Mrs Y and the Year 1s. She was wonderful and understanding. I realised too that my preferred age group to work with were KS1 children.

I also worked in the after-school kids club. That brought back memories of Tenerife. I met some great people, too: FA, AB, CY, AG, NR, RG, AH and LH. I loved working with the kids and helping them in their studies, but also interacting with them in the playground and in kids' club, which reminded me of when I used to go to a play centre myself. We played cards, table tennis, board games, cricket, and football. Once again, I developed feelings for a few of the teachers - AB, AG, LH and DB. But again, I didn't say anything until the end of my time there; and now they are all happy with their significant others. I really liked DB in particular, but it just wasn't to be.

The bike ride was really tricky and culminated in a steep hill, which took a lot out of me as I arrived at the school. I reluctantly decided to move on. I did return once, a few months later, to see how the teachers and kids, now a year older, were getting on. I stayed the whole day, getting involved. It was lovely to see that many of the children remembered me.

After finishing at WFIS in the summer of 2016, I had to make the daunting trek to the Job Centre again. This time, however, they were a lot more accommodating: now aware of my specific needs. Although I didn't have much success finding a placement, I did, through the local charities, find a position at a library shop in Epsom. I did not start straight away though as we were moving home again. Before we moved, Mum had gone to the pub where she saw an adorable dog. The owner offered her the dog and she took it. Replacing Henry was difficult. But Ollie is one of the loveliest dogs ever. He gets my brother and me through some difficult times. Poppy has always done that too, but it was nice to have two again. So anyway, in 2016, we moved from Danetree to Eastdean, which was slightly closer to town.

The change of environment was difficult for me and my brother, but it was a nice house and, for the first time in my life, I had my own room. Upsettingly, though, our previous landlord refused to return our deposit because they claimed we hadn't cleaned the house properly. I found this disgraceful. My mum had worked so hard to get it back to the condition it was in when we had moved in. For the next two years or so, she fought to get the deposit back. She didn't get it, and that was devastating for the family.

Despite all the changes, I was starting to feel a bit better about myself and was starting to push myself out of my comfort zone. Throughout the year, I tried to be more active and social again by visiting friends from all walks of life. I went to Waterloo to meet my one-time crush HP and also met up with the Lynches, from my time in Tenerife. HP is now married and despite choosing AC over her (due to distance), we became good friends, and she has always been so wonderful and supportive. I'm glad she is part of my life. I met her in the morning, and we spent around three hours in Waterloo before she had to go. I then called CL and we met up and spent the rest of the day together. That was such a great way to start the year. I did this several more times throughout the year, seeing BD and RC, and hanging out in Central London, meeting SF and going to Piccadilly Circus, and LM from summer camp and spending time with her and her friends in Hyde Park, and getting together with EK and my best friend SC in Epsom. All these occasions helped me improve my confidence.

With the change of scenery, I also decided to try the world of online dating again. Similar to the previous time, most were ignorant: they either catfished or led me on before disappearing. I did meet two really nice people though and met up with them. First, fellow dog lover LS. We decided to take our dogs for a walk on Epsom Common for an initial meet-up. She showed up with a special car that carries dogs in the back. We got on really well. But after we hugged and said goodbye, I received a text a few days later saying she was moving away, which was upsetting. She said it had been in the pipeline for a while but was confirmed when her mum had said it was officially happening. Truth be told, she disappeared after that, which was a shame, but understandable as she had moved to a new home and started a new life.

I went back to the drawing board and came across EM, another lovely girl. She has, from day one, been inconsistent with regards to messaging but we have so much in common - and that was evident from our initial interactions. In a rare moment, I agreed to a phone call. Although she did most of the talking, we spoke one night for more than five hours! As the months passed, we agreed to a date in Kingston. We got on really well. I met her outside a Costa. We walked for miles. It was really nice as we got to know more about each other, and I feel that, despite the recent absence, we are still good friends. I do also feel we liked each other but she is a very busy individual with work and family, and the distance become difficult. So, it was just the one date. I still care about her a great deal - and she's the only person I've ever met from El Salvador.

As 2016 was ending I pushed myself to go to Comic Con with my brother. This was a busy and hectic day. We were on our feet for most of it. My brother even went in cosplay, as a robber from the game Payday. It was an incredible occasion. I got a photo and autograph of the amazing John Noble, the Australian actor who plays Dr Walter Bishop in Fringe, one of my favourite TV shows; a great moment for me. I waited in line *twice* to see him. As I approached to get his autograph. I said it was an honour to meet him. It took a lot of guts to come to the event and Fringe had got me through some difficult times. I told him this, and he asked about it. I said shows like Fringe gave me an escape from the world and distracted me from negative thoughts - and frankly kept me going. He signed the picture and shook my hand. He said well done for coming and wished me all the best. It was a great day, seeing all the cosplayers, all the memorabilia - and getting my photo taken in the DeLorean dressed as Marty McFly from Back to the Future.

As the year ended, I felt that things were starting to improve. Mum and Nan were starting to patch things up. However, we were about to lose another significant family member. Granny Kath died and it was another devastating occasion. I could not push myself to go to another funeral. Not after my previous experience. So I stayed home with my brother.

Despite being in a better state of mind, I still wanted to find out why I am like I am, which took me back to the G.P. The current medications clearly weren't working so we switched them. I was put on another waiting list to get CBT again and tried anything to stop feeling the way I was feeling. I was clearly still struggling, despite what had mostly been a better couple of years. But I kept pushing forward for my loved ones.

Above: At Comic Con, 2016, and below, from the same year, gaining Level 2 certificate in support work in schools.

CHAPTER 12

THE QUIET LIBRARY, THE WAKEUP CALL AND E.G.H

THE placement in the Epsom LIBRARY shop was again an escape for me. Just one day a week, while the rest was filled with caring for my brother and seeing loved ones - especially HW. I saw her often and had some great times with her. She came to my house a lot. We watched TV and played video games and went for a drive in her car now and again. We went to restaurants, the park (which was when I opened up and told her everything) and more meetup events throughout the year. She has changed my life for the better.

Tee-Jay and I were still going on dog walks, cycling, playing tennis, and popping into town, to break the monotony of being stuck at home playing video games. By now he had a support worker. No longer with us due to moving away, twice a week he took my brother out for a few hours. He helped Tee-Jay progress and had such a positive impact on his weekly routine. So much so that Tee-Jay refused to do similar with any other support worker. There was a great rapport and friendship built through him and the family and all were all sad to see him go. Izzie had also found a passion for playing video games (it didn't last). As I had my own room for the first time, I was able to have people visit me without my brother feeling uncomfortable. So, Izzie came in often to play with me on the Wii U, games like Rayman Legends, Mario Kart and Mario Party. I also invited HW over as often as possible. Those visits provided much needed company as my isolation was becoming more intense. I virtually felt like a prisoner in my home.

I started the year trying to catch up with EP, an old friend from university who has had similar difficulties to me. She is a wonderful person with a heart of gold. This day out in London was exactly what we both needed. Once again, I pushed through my anxiety barriers to get on the train to Waterloo, wanting to see someone I really care about. We strolled down the Thames Path, dropped into the Tate Gallery and also attended a special event in the Southbank Centre - EP, who has a love for poetry, took me to a library I never knew existed. It was a wonderful day and knowing she lived in Ipswich, I was all too aware I may not see her again for a while, so gave her a really long hug goodbye. She is a wonderful friend and we really do support each other with our respective difficulties.

Once settled in Eastdean, I set about my tasks at the Epsom library shop, a role that lasted about four months before I looked for paid work. Now closer to town, I was able to walk to the library instead of cycling or taking the bus, and this helped my brother and I. Arriving on my first day I was shown around. The shop lay in the far corner of the library and was filled with books and stationery and a desk with a cash register, where I would be working. I only worked with two people in my period at the shop and they had similar difficulties to me. It was clear from the off that I wasn't particularly enjoying this job, mainly because it was a pretty quiet environment - on a good day we'd have around 10 customers. However, I did enjoy meeting a lovely colleague, who was around 30 years older than me. I had a massive wakeup call seeing him and talking about our lives. He had worked there for a couple of years and did not look particularly happy. I realised at that point that I did not want to end up like him, and this ultimately persuaded me to visit a jobs fair in town. The actual job itself gave me anxiety too, especially on the days I worked alone and had to operate the till while the customers waited to pay for their purchases. Often, though, I just sat there waiting for someone to come in, so I'd distract myself with puzzles and so on. I met some nice people there, but it really wasn't for me.

The day I braved the jobs fair was another filled with anxiety. I traipsed from stall to stall, but nothing really appealed until I came across Epsom Hospital's stand. I took some leaflets and pored over them. I came across several roles I thought I'd like to try but the one that stood out to me was a hospital porter job, which would combine helping people and possibly working with children. I applied and got an interview. I was absolutely terrified. Interviews scare me. But I took a deep breath and was my usual open and honest self. The interviewers were very impressed, however, they said that most starters in this environment begin in admin work. I was reluctant at first but I decided to give it a try. One of the interviewers told me that I should be really proud, which definitely made me feel better about myself going forward. I had to undertake numerous training courses, mostly online, and didn't start at the hospital until a few months later.

Once more I was starting to feel better about myself. Typically, however, that optimism didn't last. I had another breakdown. I just felt surrounded by negative media. I felt so alone too, like I was losing all my friends and family. Then there was the endless frustration of not knowing why I am like I am. It was inevitable. The kicker, I think, was when I watched news reports on two major tragedies that year. The first one was the Grenfell Tower disaster, the Kensington flats that caught fire killing 72 people; it was devastating to see. It was made worse when I saw friends suffering because they knew people involved in the tragedy. The second was the suicide bombing at Ariana Grande's concert in Manchester. This one really hurt me. I stayed up until the early hours feeding off endless updates. I watched a Jason Manford live-feed, which was heart wrenching, seeing things from the comedian's viewpoint, with him declaring he'd had enough of seeing things like this happen. An opinion I share.

As a consequence, I decided not to watch the news anymore; it just tears at me. There is frankly more bad news than good, and it is not how it should be. These days it is almost impossible to completely avoid the news, particularly because of the prominence of social media. As much as I care (probably too much), I can't deal with all the negativity anymore.

When those old feelings re-surfaced, I went back to the GP. I laid out everything. But shockingly, I was told that my diagnosis was not in fact official; that broke me mentally. I immediately requested I be put on the waiting list to be assessed. I also wanted to change medications as they clearly were not working. And I asked to have CBT again; I really needed more support.

Mum had an up and down year too. Having left John, she turned to online dating and met MP who lived in Chelmsford. It was a crazy number of months. The distance was too much, and Mum struggled to balance family, work, and her relationship - my sister wasn't particularly fond of him - and after a few months it became too much for them both. Then mum met Dan Brooks. And I'm happy to say they are still together. As usual, it took me time to adjust to the change, having a new person around the house. But as time passed, I realised the positive influence Dan was having on the family, and now we have a great bond.

I remember one day Elliott coming home from work (he practically lived with us at this point). All of a sudden, I heard a scream from outside. I went to investigate and found Elliott in pain but couldn't understand why. I completely froze - which I've done before in moments like these - trying to understand the situation. Elliott, while parking his bike, had somehow caught his hand between the cycle and the wheelie bin. After gathering myself, and realising what had happened, I helped lift the bike so he could free his hand. I don't know why I freeze in situations like these. But thankfully he was okay.

Isabelle was again having difficulties at school, which was common for all of us during our school days. Summer was working at Wilsons, the Epsom car dealership. She was doing really well in life. I was still caring for my brother, trying to get us out as much as possible. We went to town, on dog walks, played tennis and took bike rides, which was great as we now lived very close to Epsom Common. I was hanging out with HW a lot this year and sometimes saw the Rotaract as well. I will always be appreciative of JB, LD and TH and many others in the group; they always made me feel at ease and I enjoyed the evenings spent with them.

August 2017, and I once again entered the world of work, taking a job in the medical records department at the hospital in Epsom. On my first day I was met at reception by AC and taken down to the basement where I was introduced to DP and JB. AC gave me a tour and introduced me to my colleagues who, over time, really became a work family. But the environment, even from the early days, was overwhelming for me. Being in the basement made it really hot, and a difficult place to work. I have an incredible level of admiration for those who work there five days a week. As with every one of my work placements, I once again struggled to fit in at first; but I was determined to try, so I hung out with my colleagues during the lunch hour and after a few months braved some work outings with them.

In the two years I worked there, I gave everything each day I was there, and it took a lot out of me, physically and mentally. I badly damaged my back and when I got home each evening, I would crash out, exhausted. Early on, I met some great people such as LJ, JS, MS, LG, and HS as well many other wonderful people who really helped me settle in and made me feel like one of them, despite only working two days a week. LJ was another who had similar difficulties to me, so I had an immediate connection with him. As the months passed, I was starting to really struggle because of everything I was trying to deal with. And, for the first time, I started opening up to the senior leaders within medical records. JB is one of the most supportive and understanding bosses you could ask for. I was offered counselling and the staff were consistently motivating and reassuring me, which I needed because I was thinking of giving up. But I stuck at it and got very good at my responsibilities, which improved my confidence and led to me being more comfortable with my colleagues, in and out of work. Towards the end of the year, I did start developing feelings for a few of my colleagues: AB, LF, GD, and for a while LG. I found out early on that GD was in a relationship, so I moved on and feel that we are now great friends. In a rare boost of confidence, I messaged AB and LF on Facebook, because it is the only way I am able to express my feelings. LF was also in a relationship, which I was unaware of, but AB wasn't. However, she had recently broken up with someone, so wasn't looking to get back into a relationship. I never actually told LG I liked her, but again we have grown into great friends. She was the first person I spoke to at the hospital, and she helped me through the early weeks. Sadly, it was more disappointment and more of what I am used to, but I didn't let it get me down.

The workplace had a revolving door feeling about it. This became more apparent during my time at the hospital. People coming and going fairly regularly. I was sad to see GD, LJ, and JS go, but it was nice seeing them off on one of our outings to the local Wetherspoons. I even spent one of my birthdays there with these lovely people, and really started to feel like part of the team. So much so that I started opening up to more people, like MN, MO, HS, and NK, who have all been really supportive and accepting of me.

That year I also had a long overdue catch-up with an old friend from Elliott School, one of my favourite people. We have been friends for more than 20 years and I'm forever grateful to have met her. She came to Epsom for a reunion, and we spent hours at the Faraday, a local bar, reminiscing and watching a Chelsea match. She opened up about issues in her family and I did the same. Some of my old feelings did surface again that evening, but sadly she was with someone so there was nothing I could do.

2018 began in a really difficult way. The wonderful EP, with whom I'd had a lovely time in London with just a year before, was in a really dark place, and after seeing a status implying the worst I was naturally panicked and on edge. As when I'd lost Ty, EP was having similar difficulties, dealing with the loss of her brother. She was contemplating ending the suffering and had gone missing. I was generally terrified and sat glued to her Facebook page for hours on end, hoping she would be found safe. I was thinking, *This can't happen three times in four years.* Thankfully, she was found and has made an amazing recovery since. I am grateful for every day I see her living her life, undertaking her passion for dancing, and becoming more and more like her old self.

I had also been struggling with my Aunty Sarah's battle with cancer over the past few years. She had recently been in remission. But during this year, the cancer returned. The family, in her eyes, had turned its back on her and aside from me she didn't feel many were on her side anymore. I adore all the family on my dad's side, but I wish more of them had been there for her during this time. I always love catching up with Sarah and my cousins Heidi, Bradley and Callum. I am so proud of the absolute genius Bradley has become. My love and thoughts are always with Sarah, and I hope to see her again soon. Coincidentally, she was friends with NR, the lady I worked with at Wallace Fields School. Seeing their similar battles with cancer, I suggested they got in touch; no person should have to face it alone.

I mentioned earlier that suppressed thoughts were becoming too much for me, so CBT could not come around soon enough. I was struggling to adjust to my new medication and starting to shut myself off from the world. I had my pre-assessment with a return to the Brickfields. I told the therapist everything I could remember, which led to me being transferred to the ASD services and receiving an official diagnosis the following year.

During what was mostly another negative year, one of the best things happened. I found out my sister was pregnant. I was going to be an uncle for the first time. But it was bittersweet as I realised my sister wouldn't be living with us for much longer. That was hard to take. Dan was moving in, and Summer was planning on finding a place for her, Elliott, and my soon-to-arrive nephew. Teddy-Ray was born on October 20th, 2018 at the hospital I work at, and Summer moved out a few months later.

The year again ended sadly as we lost Aunty Julie. We had also lost Uncle Ron in recent years, and it was devastating to see my cousins Matthew and Craig lose their parents in such a short space of time. They were a massive part of my childhood and will never be forgotten.

But I was looking forward to 2019, hoping as usual that things would get better. But after barely three years at Eastdean, we were on the move again.

We moved into our new home in February 2019, but it wasn't too much of a change as we were still in

Epsom. Unfortunately, we had similar issues with the landlord when we left our old place as we had had in the past. But this time mum had photographed the house and could show the effort she'd put in. The actual move was exhausting and took a lot out of me physically, but a lot of family members helped.

My sister Izzie, however, suffered a great deal at this time. Someone she knew had groomed and abused her. It really changed her as a person. After a lot of work, supported by the family and professionals, she is thankfully finding her way back, and is focusing again on her studies. In fact, Izzie now has a great passion for animals and is looking to work with them in some capacity.

It was a tough start to the year. And this was compounded by the reality of how far the world had fallen. I rarely watch the news, though it is frankly impossible to avoid, and on one of those occasions, they ran an item on how knife crime has increased in London. They highlighted an incident that took place on the train I regularly travel on to Waterloo where someone was killed. This was probably the moment I started becoming more agoraphobic and not really pushing myself to go out, aside from to work. At this point I felt I really was losing everyone and that I only had my family left. I had grown closer to Dan in recent months and following the months in our new home, found myself hanging out with him more. Me and Tee-Jay were once again sharing a room. However, his computer was downstairs, so it didn't really affect us.

Taking baby steps, I started to go out and about again. I went to a Chelsea FC youth match with Dan and Elliott. Later on that year, the family went on a lovely day out to Brighton. Mum, more understanding than ever about the severity of my condition and what I deal with, had been making plans to try, at least once a week, to do something together. These trips included going to Epsom for lunches, Epsom Downs for a picnic and playing some cricket and football with the family.

Brighton was a lovely day. We walked along the beach front, which brought back memories of Tenerife. We went to a Harvester, the aquarium, then had a walk around the local shops. The highlight, on a personal note, was when we went to Brighton Pier and popped into the arcade. Normally I have no luck with the claw machines. But this time, I won three teddy bears with £3, which was amazing. It was a lovely but exhausting day - and I was starting to find my way back again.

Back at work, I was starting to struggle. After a discussion with my boss, it was agreed that I could cut down to one day. I had also developed feelings for the lovely LP, who I'd pushed myself to tell how I felt about her on Facebook. It cost me. She eventually replied saying she was in the early stages of seeing someone else, which was disappointing. She is still a friend I care for greatly.

I also opened up to MN during a period of a difficult few weeks, when I was close to breaking point and close to leaving. My difficulties intensified each day because I had to walk past a local primary school to get to work. This reminded me of my desire to work in education with children.

I was really struggling, and physically - particularly with my back getting worse - it was becoming too much for me. Honestly, I would have left sooner if I hadn't developed such a fondness for everyone I worked with. But I kept going and kept giving my all to repay the patience and acceptance shown by my colleagues. As the months passed, I just couldn't do it anymore so I had a meeting with HS and JB and we decided I should become more of an on-call worker, going in only when there was a vacancy.

Truth be told, that was the last I heard from them or the workplace in general. I lost touch with several of my so-called "work family". Some removed me as a friend on social media. I had truly trusted, opened up, and left myself vulnerable to a number of these people, and it felt as if they had abandoned me, which really hurt. Coming just before lockdown, this really was the final blow when it came to me trusting others. Then the pandemic hit, and although I was already agoraphobic and fearful of the world, I now also feel lost and almost like I don't want to try again - at least in a social or work sense. In regard to work, going through the whole application process, interview, and everything involved in a working environment, after all that has happened, would be tough. On top of the decline in my physical and mental health, the thought of feeling on edge every day I go to work, giving my all, only to be thrown away and forgotten when my time ends, would be unbearable again. Struggling to socially interact and fit in would slowly make me feel worse about myself and it would continue this negative cycle of decline.

A few months ago, I went for my official ASD assessment. My mum and I travelled to Guildford. After three hours of questioning and talking about my life, the assessor said the results were inconclusive and that I needed further testing before being given an official diagnosis. The assessor said I have many traits of autism but not quite enough to be Asperger's. I do feel I am on the spectrum, but we still don't know what the specific terminology is. As I have been throughout in my life, I am always in the grey area of not knowing why I am like how I am. I know I have always had generalised anxiety disorder, clinical depression, and situational mutism, but with regards to ASD, I am still in the process of officially finding out.

Over the last few months, I have slowly become more introvert and agoraphobic, frankly in a rut. A monotonous routine of playing video games with Dan being my only real form of social interaction. It is safe to say my family and Teddy are the only things keeping me going of late, and one of the few things that put a smile on my face. I am never going to stop trying to get back to where I want to be though, and now that people are more aware of my difficulties, I am getting more support and acceptance than I've ever had.

My current medication has had hardly any positive effects, and in fact has made me feel worse, which led me to the decision to come off them again. My current medication really has had an effect on my energy levels. I am frankly almost always drowsy, emotionally unstable and on edge; I struggle with sleep and my eating habits have been affected as well.

This year I have been really isolated, even from my best friends, and after so many fightbacks this has been the hardest road to recovery. I recently came up with a good analogy to describe this never-ending battle. Over the course of my life, it has felt like an avalanche falling on top of me. The first time it is a mild amount of snow. I manage to break out and shout hooray, but by doing so, I cause more snow to fall on me. This time I have to dig myself out to get back to where I want to be. When I finally manage to break free, another noise causes an almost unbearable amount of snow to bury me deeper. This process is repeated over a lifetime, to where I find myself now. And I am trying with every ounce of strength left in me to get, once again, clear of the vast amounts of snow burying me, but as has happened so many times, I just can't quite make it to the surface. The point is, whilst I have this amazing resilience and mental toughness to keep going for my own sake and for the sake of my loved ones, there is a sense of inevitability that something down the road - a death, a negative experience, a loss of any kind - will result in another avalanche. Hence a thought of "what's the point?" fills my mind. The snow buries me, leaving me alone with no support to fight the negative thoughts, with the catastrophising every experience I face drowning me further.

But the way I have felt in recent months, I did need a new hobby. So, after people said I was better at writing than speaking, I decided to give writing a book a go.

In December 2019 a letter arrived setting up an appointment and follow-up from the ASD assessment six months prior. I was asked to attend a speech therapy assessment to gain more information and help the professionals provide me with definitive answers. I was definitely more nervous going to this one; it was another step into the unknown. But like the assessment before, Mum came with me and supported me through all of it. I wanted her to attend both assessments to truly understand all I've been through and deal with each day, and I feel the speech therapy was an eye opener for both of us.

It was another gruelling three-hour session. I was tested every which way, both my communication and general motor skills. Unlike the initial assessment, this assessor said I *could* potentially be on the spectrum. Furthermore, alongside the depression, anxiety, and situational mutism, she introduced a new condition that I hadn't looked into before. She says it's likely that I have dyspraxia. I am apparently "wired differently". I feel I have always been a good listener, but I have always had problems with retaining information, and following instructions and conversations. This applies to many aspects of life, with things varying from following directions, the flow in conversations, cooking, and education. I love Spanish, but what became apparent after reading up on dyspraxia is that although I understand the words, I've never felt fluent when listening or having conversations. When you add the speed at which they speak, I really struggle to understand it. However, when I read it, I tend to have a better understanding because I have time to process the written words.

I was given leaflets packed with information about dyspraxia, and not long after the assessment more forms arrived in the post. Although the tests eventually came out negative for Dyspraxia and ADHD, I still believe I have a number of traits associated with both conditions. I had hoped to gain much needed confirmation in 2020 so as to get the support I had been seeking for a large part of my life. I was sent another form a few months later in which I truly poured my heart out by answering all of the questions. I revealed things I'd never revealed before and, in hindsight, feel it had a huge bearing on my eventual diagnosis of ASD.

Going forward, I am still hoping to find my way back and to travel the world, hopefully helping people in different countries. I am in the process of saving up, but my conditions are holding me back from stepping out of my comfort zone again. As I write this, I am struggling to even leave my house at the moment, but with the baby steps taken in recent months I will find my way back once more and hopefully fulfil my dream soon. I am forever optimistic and determined to get back where I want to be and reach my full potential. My family, now starting to truly understand the severity of my daily difficulties and all I have dealt with, are a massive positive, and I feel more accepted, supported and understood than ever.

My nephew Teddy with the toys I won for him in Brighton in 2018.

CHAPTER 13

WHERE I AM NOW AND WHAT HAPPENS NEXT?

AFTER what has been a very challenging 30 odd years so far, I have honestly really struggled finding my way back this time. This is not a happy ending, but more one filled with optimism and a belief that things will get better once more. In the words of Winston Churchill, "This is not the end. It is not even the beginning of the end. But it is, perhaps, the end of the beginning." What I take from this is that it is never too late to start again. After what has been a rollercoaster of a life so far, this could be the end of my beginning and the future is yet to be written. So, if I keep fighting and never give up, perhaps one day soon I will get back to where I want to be.

Having said this, I have had a massive collapse mentally and physically in recent years and have also lost faith in the world. This has not been helped by the feeling of losing all those around me and this sense of isolation. I feel like a prisoner in my own four walls because I am afraid to step out into the world - I'm scared something bad will happen. The worst feeling is when I try to reach out or maintain contact with others and end up being "ghosted" and ignored by those I hold in such high regard. I think that is what hurts the most; I have so much love to give but feel it is very rarely reciprocated. In what has been a difficult life, as sad as it sounds, I've always put others first and have, over time, truly lost the ability to know how to treat myself like I treat others. I feel there has, in most part, been a nasty element to many of my friendships and relationships. I feel people at first tend to like me, grow close to me, and develop an understanding of who and how I am. But then, after a while, they turn on me and let me down before eventually removing me from their lives, when all I've ever had is good intentions.

I so want this book to have a happy ending. But as I say, that might be overly optimistic. Arguably, I feel the worst I have ever felt but take solace in the fact that I will never stop trying. I never stop wanting to find my way back, and despite feeling like an empty vessel waddling through life I still have so much to give. For me, the world has crumbled so much, and humans are the worst species to live with. There is too much hate and misery, and it is very rare you see positive stories in the news nowadays. Somebody has been shot, a bomb went off, another knife crime. This all just has to stop. But the sad reality is, in this era of social media and the internet, it is almost impossible to avoid the news entirely. We have to be better. For all the good things technology has added to society, it has also destroyed the world we live in.

How do you explain to everyone that you are in this grey area? You don't want to be here anymore, but you don't want to die either. As a result, I feel so empty and unable to barely do anything. Always lacking in energy and emotionally unstable, I am feeling lost right now as I write this. I'm afraid to leave home, go to work, socialise; and I honestly don't know how to break out of this. I have even isolated myself from my best friends. But I know, despite my personal difficulties, that I love and appreciate them all - I love you all, if you are reading this! A lifetime of dealing with my conditions and negative experiences has caught up with me, but I will not let this beat me.

Despite the negatives, I will never stop trying to get back to the person that achieved the wonderful things described in my story so far. The person who, while working abroad, was so close to reaching his full potential. The person who dreams of travelling the world and helping others in any way they can. The person who hopes to one day work in education or healthcare with children, to give them the support and encouragement that I never really received. Having just one of the conditions I have is hard enough, but to be a high functioning autistic individual, to see the world for what it really is, and people for who they really are, and to not be able to do things other people accomplish with ease... it is too much to handle.

So, what is the grand plan and what happens next? It is a really good question and one I am not fully sure of myself just yet. In the short term I want to get back to being a good carer and being more involved with my family. In fact, we surprised my sister with a break to Disneyland Paris for her 16th birthday. After a lot of deliberation, I decided to go, although as the day edged closer, my anxieties and worries continued to escalate. I realise it is unusual: most people look forward to holidays and getting away. For me, however, and my differently wired brain, I am always over thinking and worrying about every detail. What do I pack? Is everything organised and structured correctly? Will I be the good and positive company my family deserve? Are all the travel arrangements correct? And so on, and so on. The reality is that at this point in 2020 I had only been out of the house twice; so to suddenly thrust myself onto a plane once more and spend three or four days away from my safe space was quite terrifying.

On 19th February 2020, after giving Isabelle this truly wonderful surprise, we set off in the early hours to Disneyland. Prior to leaving I was on edge: for the first time in a long while I would be outdoors for a prolonged period. Suffering from all forms of motion sickness made this a very challenging few days for me, but I was determined to get through this for my little sister and nephew, and the rest of the family. The journey to the airport was exhausting, from the drive to the airport, the airport transfer, all the security checks and waiting to board. When we finally did get on the plane and it took off, our flight was less than an hour.

Arriving at Charles de Gaulle Airport, which is a maze, there was a lot more walking to be done after checks and claiming the baggage. We were indecisive about the transport we should take to the hotel, so we looked around for the best option. We opted for a special Disney express coach, despite the fact it's the worse mode of transport for me as it causes me awful motion sickness. At this point I had been out the house two times during the year, so this was a lot to handle, from the droves of people to the endless walking and anxiety with security checks. In fact, my family were not aware of this, but for almost the entire time we were in France - exacerbated by "beware of pickpocket" signs everywhere - I hardly ever let go of my wallet and phone, so my hands were always in my pockets.

I was shattered but relieved when we arrived at our hotel. We unpacked and had a few hours rest before we headed to Disney Village. The village is a free section of Disneyland full of shops and restaurants. This gave me a sneak preview of how much of a challenge the two full days in the Magic Kingdom would be, both physically and mentally. We had to go through more security checks when we were there, which further corroborated my opinion of how much the world has fallen. The place itself, however, gave me lovely memories of my time in Orlando and seeing Planet Hollywood and all the Disney shops. After getting the lay of the land, we chose to keep it cheap and cheerful and had McDonald's that first evening. After we had eaten, we called it a day; we were tired after all the travelling. As we left, we saw more security guards, some of whom were armed. This was a devastating sight for us; the last thing families should see after a day in the fantasy world of Disney.

We all slept badly and some of us were ill, which put a dent in the days to come. As always, my brain refused to switch off and listening to the other's snoring or being sick made it so difficult to get a good night's sleep. Finally, I put my headphones on and watched my shows. It's the best distraction for me. I stayed up for a while until gradually drifting off on an uncomfortable bed.

We woke up after a difficult night and went to breakfast. The hotel food was very up and down in terms of quality, but we all stuffed ourselves, fully aware of the day we were about to face. Our first of the two days at Disneyland Paris was affected early on because Dan became too unwell to come with us, so it was just the six of us. We entered the park, awed by the amazing sites and tried to forget everything. At least we hoped to forget everything. But I received a message from my bank saying there had been suspicious activity on my account. Naturally, I couldn't get that out of my head. After calling them and saying it was taken care of, I tried to get on with my day.

This day was about Isabelle's sweet 16 and Ted's first holiday abroad. We saw Goofy and lined up for the photo and to get a signature for Isabelle's special autograph photo frame. A staff member handed my sister a mobile phone. Mickey Mouse was on the line to give her a birthday message. Although there were dozens of Disney characters to see, the first day was about getting our bearings, getting on the rides and gaining memorable photos and experiences for the family.

Much of the day involved walking and taking in the spectacular views and wonders of Disneyland, visiting the shops, and acquiring "fast passes" for the best attractions. The clear favourite was Space Mountain, which was just as good, if not better, than I remember when I went there previously. Indiana Jones Adventure, which I didn't get to go on myself, was not as good as it once was, according to the others. We took so many nice pictures. Ted went on his first ever ride: It's a Small World, the water-based boat ride. And we enjoyed the parade as a family - that's what it was all about.

However, by this point I was becoming physically and mentally overwhelmed: big crowds, lights and sounds, and my back was really giving way. I had to sit down at every opportunity. I had given everything I had to get to this point and was really drained. We went to a cafe for a hotdog and then to get ready for the evening ahead.

This is when it got harder. When night fell, the rain started to pour and the weather turned colder, which meant we sadly missed out on seeing the fireworks. My family have got incredible energy and just don't know when to stop, which was evident during both days at the park. We visited a few more shops before heading back to the hotel to check on how Dan was doing. Summer had also been unwell the night before but, as she said, being a parent, you just need to find a way to keep going. I think Elliott, her and my mum are all incredible parents.

Back at the hotel, I had nothing left and had started feeling sick myself. The family went to the bar for dinner, but I couldn't move so stayed behind. I couldn't eat but I made sure I had plenty of fluids. Mum came back with a pizza but as much as I wanted to, I just couldn't eat it. I fell asleep early, aware that I would have to go through it all again tomorrow.

Our second morning was very similar but didn't involve me as I'd woken up still sick and unable to move. The family went to breakfast and brought back some brioche for me. Mum and Dan had only booked a ticket for one day, so they went to a shopping district, whereas the plan for the rest of us was to go to Disneyland for day two. Not me, though. I felt awful. So, I stayed in bed to recuperate while Summer, Elliott and Isabelle went to the park and Mum, Dan and Ted went shopping.

The clock was ticking on our last day in Paris. I kept thinking to myself, I can't waste this day. It got to about 2:30pm and I decided to join them in the park. I just hate letting people down, so I got ready and headed out. I went to the Sleeping Beauty Castle, right in the middle of the park, and waited to meet up with them all. They had been filling up the photo frame with autographs and meeting more Disney characters, getting the full experience. I feel I made the right decision. I don't think in my state I would've been able to complete two full days at that park. The funny thing is, on the second day I didn't go on a single ride. But as I said, it was more about the experience, and for Isabelle and Teddy.

We were exhausted and left the park at about 6:00pm, aware of the 4:00am wake up for our flight. We got back, reunited with the others, and had a little walk into town. On the first evening, Dan and Elliott had stumbled across a nice little restaurant. We decided we would go there for a proper meal. It was a really friendly place with great food. We were all so tired, but this was a nice way to end our break.

After an evening of little sleep again, we got the cab to the airport. However, motion sickness took over and, having felt rough from the previous evening, I really struggled with the entire journey home. Overall, I was very proud to have overcome all the fears and challenges that came with this break, but without my family I don't think I would've been able to get through it. They are everything to me and I'm grateful every day for them.

A few weeks after our Paris trip, something unprecedented happened: a pandemic. Had we gone a few weeks later, Coronavirus could have meant we ended up stuck in France. I'm not going to go into huge depth regarding my experiences during the pandemic, but I'd like to share my thoughts and perspective on the whole ordeal.

Early March, a few media outlets reported an outbreak of a disease they called Coronavirus. It didn't have a great effect on me early on, but once football matches started being postponed, it hit home. Sport has always been one of my big distractions so not having that to watch has been difficult. Of course, I tend to avoid the news. Too sad, too painful. But I was forced to face it again to get clued up on what was happening, unaware of just how serious this situation was going to become. As time passed, more and more things were either being cancelled, shut, or postponed as the world as we knew it came to a halt. That feeling alone was quite surreal; I'm sure for everyone - we had lost the freedom to do fundamental things like going shopping, meeting friends, things we usually take for granted.

At first, not much changed for my brother and me; we are mostly introverted and were only going out occasionally anyway, and I was just getting over all the difficulties of recent months, what it took to go to Paris and falling back into my agoraphobic and introvert lifestyle, when this hit. Initially, I agreed with my mum, that it was like something from a movie, it couldn't actually be real. However, once I started watching the news, seeing the rising number of infections and deaths,

I felt broken by it. As you know, I am very sensitive and things like this do take a lot out of me. While watching with Mum, I just felt empty, unable to say anything, almost choked up. I held back tears and sat there powerless to express how I felt, and when I was asked how I was feeling, it was a very minimal response. I feared the worst when I heard of the outbreak - and it didn't get any better when I was preparing to watch the Sky miniseries, Chernobyl, about the 1986 nuclear disaster.

As I write, we are still under lockdown, still in the grips of the pandemic. Our lives have come to a standstill. Extroverts have now become introverts. The economy has crashed. But we have also given the earth time to heal.

I'd like to share a status I posted very recently about my thoughts on this:

> I find it wild how people have been since this pandemic has begun. For introvert types like myself this has been my way for a while now due to my growing fear of the world and declining mental state. Yet, a week stuck indoors and all this animalistic, almost primitive behaviour from the minority has happened. I really hope this in the long run brings us all closer. A break from the world is possibly what we needed.
>
> Ever the optimist, having a global reset, we hopefully start treating each other better and try to

> make this world more united. It's wishful thinking but something has to change. The NHS are incredible as are anyone working through this difficult time to help their fellow man. I'm proud of my former work colleagues and all at the hospital.
>
> I love you all and hope you and your families are keeping safe! Xx

I feel this portrayed my thoughts once I realised just how real and severe this had become. I was fearing for loved ones. I was fearing for everyone as the numbers continued to rise. Thousands dying. More infected. I was also dismayed at the response of the few who chose to stockpile and resort to irrational behaviour to secure hand sanitizer, toilet roll and other necessities we have for so long taken for granted. By now you are aware of my current opinion of humans and how cruel we can be, and this pandemic cast a light on that.

When we entered lockdown, I was still in a bad way, even after pushing myself to go to Paris. But lockdown took so much out of me. We had eight people in our home. My sister, her partner, my nephew, as well as the five of us, all under the same roof, our movements curbed. My family are everything to me, but this became an overwhelming situation. Although my routine was quite monotonous it was definitely affected: my sister and her family took over the living room, which is where I normally go to escape from my room, where I watch my shows to avoid the world. There was so much moving of things and people to accommodate them. The worst thing personally is, I struggle with five of us: the socialising, the interacting. But now we were eight. Frankly, it was overwhelming most of the time. So much so that each morning when I woke up, I had to force myself to go back to sleep or just stay in my room. I wanted to sleep more to help the day go faster with less need for interaction and to give my brain a break. So essentially, in a time of social distancing and isolation, I barricaded myself in my room, at least until the early afternoon.

For the rest of the day, when I pushed myself to go downstairs and actually eat something, I spent time either with Elliott or Dan playing Call Of Duty or the latest FIFA football game. I felt myself questioning everything I said or did like: "should I take a bath as there are seven others here?"; "should I have a bit more food or is that being greedy?". My brain is always in overdrive and now I had to constantly think: what is best for everyone else? We always had dinner as a family though and tried to keep ourselves in the know about any developments regarding the outbreak.

April, as I said, is a difficult month. It's when I lost Ty. In the midst of the pandemic, it was especially hard. I struggled during the week of the anniversary of her death, alone with my thoughts, unable to open up to anyone about it. Every year since her passing this has been the case. But I have recently seen on social media pictures posted in support of different things. For men, it was about suicide awareness and that 75 percent of those who take their life are male. For women, it was posting a photo to build each other up instead of taking each other down. The first week of April is one I just can't forget. Even seven years after she passed, I get particularly low and shut myself off from everyone. To be reminded of how we lost such a wonderful person fills me with sadness.

When you add to this all that was happening around us due to Coronavirus, I was really struggling. This was made worse when just a few, short weeks later I lost a family member to it. Although I didn't know Charlie particularly well, I am close to his wife June. We are in regular contact and help and support one another with our respective difficulties and conditions. It was devastating seeing June lose her husband to this disease. Charlie is how I'm related to the Whitbys/Piercys, so I feel I lost that connection to them. If that wasn't hard enough, just a week later, I received news that Carmen, a member of my extended family, had incurable cancer. She has been a big part of my life so hearing this genuinely broke me. When we all lived in Roehampton we saw a lot of each other and, as I've said before, I have a few extended family members who mean the world to me, so this deeply upset me and made this pandemic and period of isolation that bit more unbearable.

As always, I suppressed and dealt with things in my own way. When I was told about Charlie and Carmen, there were others in the room with me and the news was on in the background. I just sat there on my phone in silence, trying to take in all this devastating information and fighting back the tears; trying to keep strong; pushing forward as I always do. I seek a place of silence or solitude to take in the information; I suppress it and sit there with regret and that sense of loss. I realise life and death is the way it is for all of us. But whenever I'm confronted by it, it kills me inside. I do fear that suppressing my feelings will end badly, possibly another breakdown. But I don't know how to deal with my emotions.

I continued to keep myself distracted with my TV shows, video games and even making a few new friends such as EJ and IM, who have both been wonderful and supportive. A few of us continued to work through lockdown, such as Mum, who is a carer for Surrey Council, and my sister too. Dan works for Wandle, a company that supports people across South London who need a home.

This brings me to another big thank you: to everyone who worked through this ordeal, from the

NHS to the key workers and any other person who risked their lives to keep us all safe. I thought the one-minute applause was a lovely touch, but NHS workers deserve so much more than what they receive.

That being said, I was disappointed, despite warnings from those trying to keep the nation safe, in a minority who continue to show ignorance and apathy towards the severity of the pandemic. Their inability to listen prolongs the suffering of the masses and increases the duration of this lockdown. Despite the daily increase in infections and deaths across the globe, a few are not sticking to the guidelines. People have loved ones they are missing yet follow the rules. But people going to the park in droves, crowding on the tube, generally disobeying the rules put in place for our benefit, are not only putting massive pressure on the NHS and key workers across the country, but they are also putting themselves and others - including their own families - at risk. They are also consequently adding to the length of this lockdown, and people who are so accustomed to being active and outgoing are forced to stay indoors slowly losing their minds.

My family are predominantly extrovert and busy bodies, so they were getting a little stir crazy as time passed. Teddy, for example, is like an energiser bunny: he wants to be out and about and not holed up at home. But we stuck together as a family; it's what we always do, through thick and thin. All doing our part, like so many others, as we navigate this situation.

I was supposed to be getting my diagnoses results this month (March 2020) . Frankly, I need answers before I'm able to move forward with my life. I need to understand everything and get long overdue support if I'm able to rise from the bottom once more. I had signed up for online CBT prior to Paris and undertook four sessions. Although the therapist was lovely, it was nice to actually think before I typed a response. When speaking face to face there is more pressure for me and a requirement to be more immediate in a response. Due to the pandemic as opposed to being face-to-face or on the phone - I just don't feel this kind of help works for me. I love having someone listen without fear of judgement, and actively empathising, trying to offer me support and advice on what to change. However, it just isn't for me.

My family, as ever, have been my rock and I don't know what I'd do without them. I may always be fighting an inner battle they can never truly comprehend, but they love, support, accept and stay patient with me, which is forever appreciated. This pandemic has truly tested every one of us. And despite my negative opinions of humans, we are resilient and come together in dark times.

Looking forward, I want to think about prioritising family and friends who make me feel better about myself and make more time for them. I want to find a routine that is not too overwhelming or strenuous and continue saving up for my next big adventure. I have always had so much love and empathy for others, so frankly I just don't have the heart to delete or block anyone from my life. As a result, I don't know who my real and true close friends are, or who to prioritise. Another negative of social media is that it gives you an illusion of how many people care and reciprocate the love you have for them. You may have 2,109 friends but only 10 percent or fewer really do care and make an effort. As I enter my 32nd year on this planet, I want, if possible, to figure out the people outside of family who give back the love and respect I give to them, and actively push myself to see or speak to them more frequently. By doing that I will gain more confidence and become more outgoing and less edgy, because I will be with people who accept and understand me.

That brings me onto my dream of once again travelling abroad and seeing the world. To experience different cultures, cuisines and landscapes would be truly unforgettable and perhaps even surpass my previous adventures. I would need to take small steps to achieve this though as I am struggling to even walk to my local shops at the moment. I feel I will definitely need some company to do this, but it is something I will continually strive for. On my adventures, I hope to combine travelling and couch surfing, using a company called Workaway, which allows members to arrange homestays and cultural exchanges. You volunteer a certain amount of time each day in exchange for lodging and food, which is provided by the host. So, I could give a couple of hours of labour every day for five days for food and accommodation. Then in my spare time, I will be able to explore and experience different countries and hopefully find myself again.

When I return, I guess my plans involve more down-to-earth ambitions, those most people share. Ideally, finding a partner and starting a family, finding a job I enjoy, moving into my own place, and feeling more content with my life - that would all be amazing. This will take time, but if I show the kind of attitude and determination I have done in the past, and also continue to have the support of loved ones, I believe one day I will get where I want to be.

Family photo in Disneyland Paris: Mum, Izzie, Summer, Dan, Elliott and Teddy, 2020.

EPILOGUE

THE NEVER-ENDING BATTLE WITH MYSELF — LIFE WITH MY RESPECTIVE CONDITIONS

I WOULD LIKE to start the epilogue with a Facebook status that I posted last year. I feel it puts into context how hard it can be living with my conditions:

> Dealing with mental health and the conditions I have is overwhelming and exhausting physically and mentally. I have had these for a large part of my life and daily life is such a challenge. Bluntly put, I feel unless someone does something drastic nobody truly cares and by then it is too late, and that is so wrong. I am and have been really struggling with this endless feeling of anxiety and depression, this constant apathy and ignorance others show me, trying so hard to be genuine,

empathetic and make an effort with everyone because I don't want people to suffer like I do.

People have varied opinions, but I have always tried to be good to others and be the best person I can be. I feel like I have never fit in anywhere and I blame my inability to express and communicate in any form or ask things of others a key factor. I don't think anyone understands how frustrating from my perspective to not be able to do things others find so simple. To socially interact, to go out and be active, to form and maintain friendships and relationships, to struggle to have a full-time job, to be anxious and over think everything. I realise I am pouring my heart out here but know I don't do this for attention (it's never about this). I want people from my past and present to truly understand why I am like I am and always have been.

I will never stop trying to improve, continuing to help and support my family and friends any way I can and being a good, loving and empathetic person to others. I have always been real, have no hidden agenda (actually really don't like backstabbing and two-faced behaviour), genuinely want the best for everyone and never intentionally hurt or upset anyone. I'm taking steps to rise again but with my faith, trust and confidence so low it is more difficult this time. I want to and deserve to be happy and have the things so many around me have but at the end of the day it's up to me to get there and fulfil my potential. I love all my friends and family and am proud of my achievements to date but I'm tired of hiding and frankly being treated the way I have been. I will get there... I have to.

Battling each day of my life with General Anxiety Disorder (GAD), situational mutism, depression, and a form of ASD has been, and is, emotionally and physically draining. To not have the ability to switch off mentally, to not be able to express or communicate effectively with others, to struggle with sleeping, to not feel like you fit in no matter how hard you try, to constantly feel like a failure to friends and family, to be sensitive to everything that goes wrong in your life and unable to understand the world around you and the behaviours of others, to have an endless fear of being judged, and asking for things and always fearing the worst *is just exhausting*!

With my knowledge of mental health, I understand the need for further awareness and support because there are so many like myself out there needing that help and advice to better their lives. The key is to be there for others, support and listen to them when they are in need and for sufferers to just never stop fighting. When you have truly suffered, you realise life is short and you never want anyone to face similar obstacles and pain. Having worked in a hospital for two years, I was every so often reminded when I saw older people on gurneys, of just how short life is. It's why I choose, despite all the bad experiences, to love and support everyone in any way I can. I believe in making an effort with all those who play/played a role in my life. Tell people how you feel, hug them and show you care, take photos and make memories, don't judge or belittle someone and instead be kind in all you do. Don't ignore messages and try to be the first to message. Tell people you love them because you don't know when the last opportunity will arise. There is too much evil in the world so be a shining light and prove there is more good than bad.

I have been a long time fan of Paddy McGuiness from shows such as Max and Paddy, Take Me Out, Top Gear and Question of Sport among others. In recent times, he has been publicly open about his personal difficulties, particularly his battle with depression. Furthermore, his wife Christine, through an insightful documentary named Our family and autism, discussed her and her family's issues with autism and how they handle it on a day-to-day basis. The programme received generally positive feedback, enhanced awareness on a greater scale generally and the family as a whole are now getting the love and support they deserve.

Another high-profile figure who is also open and vocal about his own autism is Chris Packham, a renowned environmentalist, wildlife enthusiast and presenter of Spring Watch. Chris has spoken publicly about how autism affects his life and presents a positive and encouraging public persona, acting as a great role model to many. He similarly released a two-part documentary recently named Inside our autistic minds which showed a true perspective of four individuals on the spectrum. It was a perfect example of 'If you have met one person on the spectrum, you have only met one person on the spectrum' showing the diversity that comes with autism in a wonderful way. The show enabled those individuals to in their own way explain to loved ones how it was for them on a daily basis.

People may say they support you and be there for you but honestly, the waiting list for professional help is ridiculous and so-called loved ones disappear and leave you to fight on your own, even when you push yourself to open up and ask for help. I feel this is truly evident when one turns to drastic measures. A perfect example came to light very recently when Caroline Flack took her own life.

Long story short, I feel the behaviour and approach to mental health, as well as other conditions, is different, and I have never understood why. I personally didn't choose to be like this so why do people constantly shun and treat me differently? What I wouldn't give to be like others around me. The world is terrifying, and I struggle to handle the way people treat each other. We have to be better, more accepting and understanding; I really do feel we are an awful species. Unless you have experienced or understood what people with mental health and ASD issues go through, you will never understand how hard each day can be and just how important kind words or any form of love and support is for people like me. I just wish things were different.

HYPER EMPATHY

This is how I've always been. The signs are: struggling to say no to others; putting your own needs last; allowing others to be unkind to you because you feel sorry for them; and, emotional responses that are out of proportion, such as bawling at a photo of an animal being hurt or feeling rage when a mother chastises a child in public.

An empathy overload can be a silent killer too. It's wonderful to care for others but it's also important to take care of yourself.

The more I think about this, the more things start to make sense. Over the course of my life, I've allowed all the positive reinforcements to sail over my head and taken onboard every negative things such as insults, experiences and criticisms, and it has become my norm, which is devastating. No wonder I'm always so mentally fatigued. I've barely woken up and I'm tired; it's not right.

I have discovered a lot from writing this book. It's opened my mind and made me at least understand myself a little better - or I'm getting there. But without help I will never know how to counteract these emotions and find a way to live my best life.

No wonder I struggle. I am taking the weight of the world on my shoulders because I care so much about everything and everyone, and it is not reciprocated.

This is a dark world. I see it for how it is since I seem to have absorbed all its negative traits. I wish it was a better place.

*

They say sticks and stones can break your bones but names will never hurt you. To me, that's awful because I feel it just as much as being hit in the face. The psychological damage it can cause is catastrophic.

Nothing will ever stop bullying. Sadly, it will always exist in some form. Bullying is always present, be it online, a result of bad parents or a negative upbringing, and life being a never-ending popularity contest, and that is devastating. Humans can be awful animals. We are discriminatory for no reason. We fight and lie for power and status. We create and destroy everything. We are criminals, selfish, greedy, and I can never come to grips with any of it. I just can't see many positives anymore; it's like everyone is in it for themselves. A dog-eat-dog world, and a survival-of-the-fittest mentality.

I feel like this world has stolen my naive belief that there is good in everyone. There isn't, I know now. Certain people are horrible. They want others to suffer. These criminals, these racists, there is no legitimate reason for what they do. We shouldn't need campaigns like Black Lives Matter or #MeToo because it's common sense, surely, that we are all the same and deserve to be treated as such - in our one opportunity on this planet. It's all just so messed up. We are just an awful species. Somebody needs to say this.

*

During my life I have repressed so much; it has led to numerous breakdowns. I don't think Summer, my sister, understood the magnitude of what I have dealt with/have to deal with until she read this book. I used to be intimidated by her. Other family members were "tough-love" types. And when I'm under pressure, when the spotlight is on me for example, I don't react well. Summer and Mum are the two family members I am most likely to open up to. I was watching Love Actually recently (I love this film - parts of it were filmed at my school) but I think it definitely gave me false hope when it came to relationships and friendships. I would adore to have someone to watch Love Actually with. The loneliness I feel when I see all those storylines is hurtful. It never happens to me.

Maybe, although I don't currently believe it to be the case, the best is yet to come!

Social media and online friends

Over the last few years, it has been a relatively common theme: friends and family have said I should tell my story in some way. Some have called me inspiring; some have abandoned me, not understanding how much I have dealt with. You must understand, I never do any of what I do, or have done, for attention. In fact, it is quite the opposite: I want others to receive the attention they deserve and need, particularly those suffering alone with mental health and ASD, not knowing what to do or where to turn. After a number of years of delaying, due to the fact I didn't like writing, I decided to give it a try. I am not expecting this to be a best seller, but if I can help improve the life of *one* person, I will consider this book a success.

In this age of social media, I have never cared about "likes" or any form of attention from others, but I have always cared about acknowledgement of existence and not being ignored by supposed loved ones, who at one point were a big part of my life. It may be a cliché, but we really do only live once and I treasure the part – big, small, positive or negative - anyone in my life has played. So, when they ignore, "ghost" or even delete me from their life, it hits me hard. I just don't understand:

is it really that hard to reply to a message or make a mutual effort? I get that personal lives and busy lifestyles can have an effect, but anybody can take a minute out of their day to maintain contact with another.

With all of this in mind, the deciding factor with regards me writing this book came strangely in the form of a dream just a few of months ago. Although I have had several dreams with potentially good ideas, I forget them quite soon after waking up. This dream was different though, and I decided that once I woke up, I would write down what I had dreamt. The initial intention before writing this book was a film, featuring myself alongside fellow sufferers, and in a strange way my two ideas now coexist. I named the movie Somebody Has To Do It - End The Stigma, End Discrimination, End Crime and this is what I wrote, with some recent changes, following my dream.

PLOT

The story revolves around a trio of strangers (two white and one Asian) who become friends dealing with different forms of abuse and discrimination in a rough neighbourhood in Ireland. Each story is told individually with overlaps from the other two (all in the same college). One, a female, has an abusive father; she is physically bullied at school due to being overweight and has an eye patch due to an infection early in life.

The second is a foreign exchange student trying to start over after growing up in a third world country. His parents over the course of his early life save up enough money to send him off to college with the hope of him leading a better life. In his adolescence, he is still figuring out his sexual orientation and the surrounding issues, and in college he is racially abused and endures further bullying (featuring subtle interactions and overlaps with the other two main characters). This builds up over time until he can't take anymore and retaliates in dramatic fashion. Failing in his studies and tired of his maltreatment, he is kicked out of school after putting the bully in hospital. With minimal income and unable to find work, he ends up on the streets and turns to alcoholism and self-harm.

The third is loosely based on my life. This individual has serious mental health issues after the loss of a friend to suicide. The friend was a victim of cyber bullying that went too far. With the early break up of his parents, bullying throughout school, and never understanding why he didn't fit in, he is diagnosed with autism later in life, although this is not known within this story. He sees the world for what it is and has lost faith in humanity, seeing more bad than good in what he deems 'the worst species.' Despite having a wonderful family around him, he is desperate to seek answers as to why people treat him the way they do.

Each story is shown individually before they all reach tipping point and meet at a church support group. The foreign exchange student now volunteers at the church and notices the other two from school. They decide enough is enough and formulate a plan with the intention to change the world for the better. After many rejections from figures in the entertainment industry they turn to social media. They create a group, which is received with moderate success. They find more members to join the cause and form the tagline, Somebody has to do it.

The foreign exchange student is taken in by the mental health sufferer and his family, after a long conversation with his mother. The mother happens to work in the mental health industry and puts him in contact with the relevant professionals to help him to come off the drink and stop self-harming. One member of the Somebody has to do it group has connections with a TV producer, and they get an appearance on a prime-time chat show. In a moving speech, several of them share their stories, covering a wide range of topics and helping increase awareness of all the negative sides of humanity. They finish by chanting Something has to change and We all need to be better. The audience agree and applaud the young adults' bravery however, nothing really changes, and the show is met with mixed reviews.

The trio don't give up, but the foreign student is attacked and murdered after walking home from the church in a 'mugging', when in reality it was the bully fresh out of the hospital with his big brother who stabs the foreign student after an altercation. It transpires the bully didn't know of his big brother's intentions and they both flee the scene. He goes down as a martyr by the other two and becomes the face of Somebody has to do it.

The other two, crestfallen by recent events, make one final attempt to succeed by creating a movie summarising all that is wrong with the world featuring their own stories. A film company loves the concept and gives the two an opportunity. The film premiere ends with a memorial of their fallen friend and a standing ovation, with a substantial level of awareness of the issues raised fulfilled by the movie's success and people gaining a greater understanding of how bad humanity can be in terms of discrimination, crime and abuse.

After the film's success there is a brief spell of peace and tranquillity, with viewers humbled and empathetic towards the cast. A montage is then shown of the good in humanity e.g. giving to the poor, helping the elderly across the street, showing affection instead of hurt and bullying, and even a scene of the bully changing his ways after seeing the actions of his big brother (and its consequences) and replacing the murdered student by volunteering in the church.

However, this doesn't last and although the movie affects a portion of the population positively, the majority are unaffected, proving how much humanity has fallen. In what is not the happiest of endings, the final scenes show the female lead experiencing continued abuse from her father, leading her down the path of drugs. The remaining male lead, realising his futile attempt in changing the world and suffering from the loss of his friend that he and his family took in, shuts himself out from the world. He becomes agoraphobic, stops watching the news, his depression and anxiety increase, and he isolates himself from the world. After a long battle and a time jump, he finds his way back and decides to write a book under the same heading as the group. The film shows a book being flipped through with a number of blank pages in it indicating that our futures are yet to be written and it isn't too late for us to change. As the character closes the book the screen cuts to black. In the end credits, all things wrong with humanity are highlighted including money, crime, class systems and treatment of others, discrimination, treatment of animals, pollution, poverty, corruption, war etc. Post credits we see the full cast repeating the tagline as the reality is something has to change. We must all work harder to make the world a better and happier place.

I am sharing this with you as I did to certain friends on social media. The response was mostly positive, however, one of my best friends suggested instead of making a movie to write a book based on my own life experiences. After some thought, I agreed and have integrated my two ideas into one with the hope that I can bring hope and inspiration to others.

This has been a long time in the making because in previous years, following my supposed diagnoses and consequent joining of pages and groups on platforms such as Facebook, I have been seeking support and telling my story to those like myself and I have been greeted with so much positivity and admiration in my openness and honesty.

I have met some of the most wonderful people online, including JY, VC, LH, JP, HR, EB, EL, JG, SF, LO, and I am so grateful to have met them when I did. I considered setting up a Facebook page/group for people with disabilities, like BC, who has a page that has grown immensely over the years. I was advised to think about becoming an advocate for mental health and ASD, but I just don't feel ready to make that kind of commitment.

I cannot thank the people I met online enough, particularly during the darkest period of my life. They have helped and supported me more than they know. I'd like to think I have shown them the same love and affection. In a weird way, I feel that they can be more supportive and empathetic than close friends. For all the negative things that come with the internet and social media, this is one particular aspect which is definitely a positive.

ALAS (All lives are special)

I have been long thinking of a way to try making the world a better place and showing the goodness in humanity. An idea sprung to me randomly one night. As people we are all born, we live and we die. Outside of family and loved ones we are generally forgotten except when you are a celebrity or somebody who left a significant imprint for good or bad. I feel it is not how it should be and I feel as we are literally all in this same boat and literally all the same species we could and should be there for each other more. We are all special and as such should be remembered in some way. Not only this but I feel people who have recently lost and need support should have an avenue to not only share their love for this person to the world but also seek support, condolences and coping mechanisms amongst each other. I came to the conclusion of a modern-day obituary through social media where people can be there for each other and through their mutual loss support each other while also sharing their stories of the recently deceased. Even just a picture and a paragraph or two of the individual and what they would like in terms of support and that way we can all be there for each other through what is our most trying times in our lives. It is something we all have to go through, and most people don't know how to react or move forward from losing a loved one. consequently, I thought this could be an outlet to share with the world the wonderful person we all never got to know, to share stories, ask for support and just bring this deteriorating, discriminative and at times cruel world more together as we really are all the same. Life is hard enough we need more love and empathy for our fellow man.

FAMILY AND FRIENDS LOSSES TRIBUTE

I thought to end my book, I would include the opinions and memories of some of the most influential people in my life. They are in no particular order, but I want people to see, despite the negative thoughts and all I deal with, that I am loved and cared for, which gives me a great incentive to never stop trying to find myself again. I will, one day, return to my old self, and I feel people like these below will help me on that journey, although my conditions will always make life a challenge.

First off, I want to pay tribute to the special people I have lost. I want them to know how much I miss them and how much they supported me in getting me to where I am today.

RIP, you may be gone but will never be forgotten.

Grandpa Ron
David Cooper
Colin Ball
Katherine Corroll
Athaya Sooksai
Andrew Krinick
Ron Corroll
Yvonne Wells

Julie Corroll
Charles Barnard
Carmen Busuttil
Paul Gayson
Jean Cooper

CB

My Son, my first born, what can I say? When you were born I was so scared, but the moment I saw you I fell in love. You were such a good baby, growing up you were perfect in my eyes. You were always happy, funny, kind, cheeky, smart and clever. We spent so much time together going to Granny's (when she lived in York) and then again when she moved to Aylesbury. I was very lucky because I had a very supportive family that helped me bring you up. Nan and Granddad encouraged me to finish school and to continue to work in the bakery (I was there for years) but growing up with you has been amazing.

I've seen you grow into the wonderful man that you are today. We have been through so much together and I wouldn't be where I am today without you. You always say, "Mum, how do you keep going, you're so strong." Luke, you are the strong one and without you, Tee-Jay, Summer and Isabelle, I don't think I would have got through some of the stuff I've been through. We are such a close-knit unit and I'm blessed to have you all in my life. I have and will always support you in whatever you want to do.

Luke, you are my hero; I love you to the moon and back. Don't ever change to please anyone else, you are who you are and you're amazing. You deserve to be happy and one day that special person will enter your life.

SB

My big brother, the kindest hearted, caring, and compassionate person you could ever meet. He has a heart made of pure gold, not a single bad bone in his body. This is something I think may be what certain people have taken advantage of... leading him down a path that he should never have had to go down.

Luke growing up, in my eyes as his little sister, was a confident, fun, bubbly and extremely popular person. I find it so difficult to understand that this couldn't be any further from the truth. I feel extremely sad to learn that Luke didn't feel the way I thought he did. In fact, he felt almost the complete opposite, which really frustrates me as he is one of the very few people in this world with such a kind heart. He deserves nothing but pure happiness and love.

I remember the day Luke decided he wanted to be a police officer... it was that day that I decided I too wanted to be a police officer, just like my big brother.

In fact, most things that Luke did, or wanted to do… I followed him in doing. I used to pretend that I liked watching Golden Balls and Deal or No Deal, even though I hated Noel Edmonds… just so that I could spend time with Luke. He truly was my best friend growing up. I don't think Luke realises just how much I looked up to him as a young girl.

To my wonderful brother Luke, uncle to my boy Teddy-Ray and brother-in-law to my lovely Elliott, we all love you so very much. We hope that you realise just how special you are.

HE

My friendship with you goes all the way back to college. In a crazy and unpredictable environment, we were lucky to be classmates. I remember when we first met, I could see you were shy, but so was I. So that made me comfy around you. You were very friendly, positive and always smiling. With so many crazy personalities around us you always got involved and you were even brave enough to play football with H.E the superstar footballer and first of his name. I will never forget that amazing goal you scored. You left everyone in total shock. From that moment, I got this Harry Potter feeling about you. I guess what I'm trying to say is, even with the shyness and anxiety, there is a spark of magic within you, and if you are surrounded by positive people, we can see a lot more of whom you really are, even if it's just a small game of football for example.

JD

I remember spending hours playing tennis with you, AK, SA and DW. My memory of meeting you is very much about spending time with someone positive who encouraged everyone to play a great game of tennis. I didn't realize you had ASD until you mentioned it - all part of your unique personality. In general, I admire your ability and efforts to stay connected with a large network of friends.

CL

We met you back in Tenerife in 2012. My daughter was attending the kids club. I'm a teacher myself and right away I noticed how fantastic you were with the children. NL loved going to the kids' club and you had a really nice caring way with them. You also made parents feel very welcome and at ease knowing their child was going to be well looked after. You provided entertainment in the evening. I remember the night I spoke to you before we left, and I wanted you to know how great you were with them and how much fun she had. We went on to book Tenerife again as we had such a good time. We then met again in London when we were over in the summer for a catch up.

MT

Luke was one of my first friends in life, living on the same estate as children playing in our local playground. I have so many memories of me & Luke. Luke is a kind, trusted & loyal friend who in my opinion is as good as family to me. A man who I am honoured to have had a friendship with for as long as we have. Luke and I have both seen tough times & fought through them & survived them like the fighters we are. Luke I am honoured to call you one of my best friends, you inspire me to keep fighting & raise awareness for autism/learning disabilities/mental health and I will always have your back; love you, brother.

SC

I first met Luke in school, it was either nursery or primary school from reception, I can't quite remember. Luke was always a shy kid and took his time to speak or play with other kids in our class or in the playground.

I remember Luke and I became best of friends. We used to walk home from school together and I will always remember walking past Greggs where Luke's mum Clare worked, and we would get free cakes. Me and Luke went all the way through both primary and secondary school together and were always in most of each other's classes. We sat next to each other in our tutor group 7MH, our table was right next to the window, and I'll always remember that because when the boiler broke down in the school during the winter it was absolutely freezing in class!

Luke had a tough time in both primary and secondary schools with certain people because he was not as confident as the rest of us, but I always stuck by him and to be honest I always will. Luke will always be my number one best mate as I've known him practically all my life. I know now Luke is going through some difficult moments in his life health wise, and I will always be there to try and help him get through it.

Some of my fondest memories of my childhood with Luke include going up to his house before school to play Final Fantasy 7 as he had completed the game and I needed his help so I could complete it too. I remember going on the school athletics meets with him, which was always great fun. Except for one time. I had not trained and tried to compete in the 1,500 metre race. I couldn't finish it and ended up being sick from exhaustion. Since leaving school we probably have not met up as much as we should have done, but we are always in frequent contact and always will be in the future. The strength and courage that this boy shows, day in day out, while suffering from ASD and more is inspiring. Especially seeing him working and living in Spain being a children's entertainer and performing on stage, something I know must have been extremely difficult for him, but he still managed to do it. Luke is a great guy, and it is a privilege to have someone like him in my life.

LM

Luke is a gentle, young Englishman, with a deep sense for team working. He was a good camp counsellor who loves children and profits from any chance to dedicate time and care to the younger generation. An experienced tennis player, good tennis coach and helpful colleague on the tennis courts during the summer of 2008, which we spent together in the specialty summer camp French Woods. This is how I met and how I perceived Luke during the summer we had an opportunity to know each other, this is how we became friends.

Then I met Luke personally for the second time in his native city London during my trip to England with my Slovak friends in autumn 2015. As I am aware of the fact that Luke had to overcome many difficult situations in his life, I always admired him for his inner strength, calmness, patience, friendliness, honesty and strong sense for struggling with the obstacles that we all have to fight with in our lives.

Luke is a real friend for me. I hope this will never change and I truthfully wish him to stay as strong and friendly as he has always been as well as hope all his future dreams will one day come true.

Best wishes Luke, thanks for being as you are!

RC

We first met in September 2008 at Roehampton University. It was great getting to know you and our friendship really grew from there on. I remember that you got me into Facebook as well so that was cool. We had a lot of fun at the tennis try outs in our first week at Uni, and who can forget those epic days at the Froebel tennis courts with you, me, BD, BO, ER & II.

I had some smashing times with you and BD during our three years studying Sports Science. I can't forget the times you, BD and I played Left 4 Dead. Loved it! Graduation was a magical day for both of us. All that hard work paid off. Both our families met each other for the first time as well.

Another awesome moment was when we met up in Waterloo and went to Arcades. That was a top day before you set off to Tenerife. Once you were back, I got to meet you in Epsom a few times. On one of the days you, me and Tee-Jay went to play tennis and basketball, which was really enjoyable.

A few years after not seeing each other, we had a great reunion with you and B.D in Putney. That was a great catch up. It was the same again a couple years later when we all had a glorious day in central London.

These are the days you live for when you get the chance to spend it with genuine mates. I've always considered you as a great friend Luke.

We've been through thick and thin and whilst it's a shame we don't get to meet each other much as we used to, our friendship never dies and I can't forget some fantastic memories we've created already.

BD

Well, where do I start? Today, I live on the other side of the planet in Asia. Here I live with my wife, and we're preparing to start a family. However, Luke still features prominently in my mind and I'm going to tell you an intensely personal story about how Luke and I became friends for life. He is, and always was, a true friend. There are some deeply personal things we've shared together, and experiences that melded us as forever close. We first met back in September 2008, when I was a misanthropic punk rock kid with bags of attitude. We met at the Freshers' Fair and struck up an immediate conversation. Our mutual support for Chelsea was a big part of why we got talking.

In the following months, we became close friends alongside R.C. Together we formed a defiant triumvirate generally having a good time. However, true crisis struck a few times in my personal life. In December 2009, I came close to death. I had a stomach ulcer that blew up inside my stomach. Long story short, I was 12 hours from death by the time I made it to a hospital close to home; sometime after the initial surge of pain that plagued me. Luke and R.C came to the flat I was staying in and were clearly concerned. They helped me to get to another hospital and continued to be there as my condition worsened.

A second defining moment occurred a short while after. In my third year, I had nowhere close enough to stay. Struggling financially, I found continuing to study increasingly difficult. Thankfully, Luke's family let me stay at their house on occasion to ease the financial burden of travelling. Without Luke's mum, I would've failed to complete my studies. I remain forever grateful. I also still retain a lot of respect for Luke's brother Tee-Jay. My wife and I are building an exciting future; one that wouldn't have been possible without Luke and his family. I am eternally grateful, brother. And whenever I'm back in the Big Smoke, I'd be glad to see my old friend.

AH

I first met Luke at a house party. I seem to remember it being a costume party for some reason. Maybe it was Halloween? Then again, we always seemed to be in fancy dress costumes, so who knows when it was! I knew instantly that there was something special about him. He was quiet and polite, which are qualities that are rare to find in a university student at a party! We became friends quickly and I found that he was much more open and relaxed when it was just the two of us or even over Messenger.

We went to a park one day and we sat for ages on the swings just chatting about life. It was wonderful to see such a shy person come out of their shell and talk freely about everything. I pushed him one night though. I insisted that he came to Brixton with me to see a rock band that I knew. And he did! I was so pleased and so proud of him. I knew that taking him out of his comfort zone was a risky business, but we ended up having a really fun night and I'd like to think that he was proud of himself for going too. Unfortunately, I didn't last long at university. I enjoyed the lifestyle more than the course I was doing, so ended up moving back home to Norfolk. This meant that mine and Luke's friendship has become more of a distant friendship, but we still contact each other frequently and I'm so pleased to see that he is powering on with his challenges. He's got this!

AG

I think one of the most enduring images I have and best examples of Luke's willpower and ability to achieve results for himself has to be a moment from the end of one of our university tennis matches (the friendly rivalry of which also served as a marker for our friendship over the Uni years!). We often had many epic, drawn out matches, usually as a result of the epic, drawn out points! It was always agonizing to lose one of these points and it is easy to be frustrated - we both definitely had moments! But what stands out for me is one particular occasion where Luke surprised me, not only by coming up with a crazy flat shot that shouldn't have been physically possible (I think I have been guilty of this too!), but by using this to successfully motivate himself into a positive mindset. He acted like a changed person the rest of the afternoon and pulled out a come-from-behind victory, I think in a final set tiebreaker. We were both exhausted from running around but it was such a fun match. I wasn't even that disappointed; I just had to grab an emergency energy snack on the way home! I imagine he had to do the same... I feel it goes to show the importance of inspiration and positive thinking though!!

DC

My family and I first met Luke in 2011 whilst on holiday in Tenerife. I had just graduated from university earlier that year and had started working. We decided to take our family away on holiday. It was the first time my youngest had been abroad. A couple of years earlier while at Uni, I was diagnosed with anxiety and depression, and it was a very dark time for me personally. At one point I was considering giving up university altogether. As the holiday approached, I began to really worry about it: what if I were bad, would the kids be okay? I needn't have worried as the kids and family had the best of holidays, which was a lot down to Luke. As part of the animation team he was absolutely fantastic with families, especially the children, and my kids loved him. We were grateful to him for making our first family holiday abroad so wonderful. It was only later that I learned Luke also struggles with his mental health. Luke and I still keep in touch and he always messages on birthdays. Luke is one of the kindest, caring and genuine people that my family and I have had the pleasure of knowing.

LC

I met you Luke while working at Wallace Field Infant School and you were a volunteer. You were quiet and reserved but you were also enthusiastic and willing to join in with everything and everyone. Your kindness and genuine love for everyone was admirable. Through Facebook, I have read and learnt about your deep struggles with anxiety and your vulnerability, but no matter how low you feel I can see how hard you try to pull yourself through and try things. You always make time for people and always have kind words. You are one of the good and sincere people in life Luke.

EB

I am so glad to have a brother like you in my life! You are an absolute legend! I knew that you were such a genuine, loving person from the second I met you! I'm so proud of how far you have come and how far I know you will go in the future.

My best memories consist of cycling at 40 mph to get home as fast as possible to get onto CO-OP FIFA with you! We were an incredible partnership and I'm sure we made many an opponent throw their controller at the wall! The best memory I have with you is visiting the mighty Dons and watching them actually win a game! What are the chances!

I'm so proud of you for sharing your story with us all! It's going to be a great read. I wish you all the best for the future! Love you brother.

HW

I've known Luke for a few years now. We first met at a Friends themed pub quiz with Epsom Rotaract. Ambitious, a trooper, and open and willing to try new things, anyone could find fun things to do with Luke, that could be mutually enjoyed, whilst spending quality time together. One of a kind, with an innate gift of kind-heartedness, Luke fundamentally wishes the best for everybody, and never fails to be supportive of others. He is one of the few people who I know I can trust, and who will always be there for me, no matter what. A good listener - impartial, understanding and respectful, thoughtful and full of empathy, I know Luke is a true friend for life.

BP

This small story reflects Luke in a nutshell. When we played football, almost every other week he would try an unnecessary bicycle kick at goal instead of keeping it simple, controlling it, and assisting a teammate.

It was incredibly frustrating if you were on his team and highly amusing if you were an opposition player!

That was until his 84th attempt where one of the bicycle kicks went in. The surprise on his face was slightly less than that of everyone else on the pitch, but this goal would not have been scored if he did not annoyingly persevere with something that “was never going to work". This approach simply needs to be replicated when dealing with the social troubles he faces.

The moral of the story is, had he not tried the bicycle kicks, when everyone thought it would be impossible to score, he would never have scored. He missed 99 percent and got something that people thought was 100 percent not possible.

He always persevered when playing football and needs to apply it to more situations. I don't think he has used it in all he has faced in his life and needs to apply this more going forward. He is someone who needs support and won't be shy to admit it, so writing this piece is rather admirable and I wish him the best.

EK

Luke has always been a sweet character. Meeting at university through an Alpha club, we never actually went into faith talks. Despite his agnostic approach I would still invite him to church. I remember Luke sharing about his life, his circumstances and achievements. I would think to myself, Wow, he has done so much, overcome so much and doesn't let anything hold him back.

What astonishes me the most about Luke is his humility as well as his care for his family and others. His sensitivity and strong and kind heart are all wonderful traits. In spite of all the challenges he has, and continues to face, he will still reach out to me, meet up and show concern. Qualities that can be so rare these days and I'm so proud of him in writing this book. It will bless so many!

GB

I met Luke during our time at university through a common group of friends. From day one he has been a fun, trustworthy and loyal friend, always ready to deliver a smile and a laugh. The constant positive energy I have felt when hanging out together needs to be underlined and taken as an example, as this is how everyone should battle the adversities that we create for ourselves or which the environment around us throws at us. Luke, you are strong. Never give up and don't stop being an example for all of us!

IL

We met in Tenerife. I still see you as Killer Queen's bodyguard in We Will Rock You who brainwashed me every show we performed in. The timid guy who pushed out of his comfort zone and performed numerous roles in front of hundreds of people varying from being a Backstreet Boy to Robin Hood: Men In Tights dancer, and performing Mini Disco for the little ones almost every night. Another thing that stands out is the numerous costumes we wore throughout our time at Las Dalias, including the Christmas Elf during the festive period and Jigsaw for Halloween! You will always be known to me as Lucky Luke. Wish you all the best and hope to see you again one day!

VC

As a mother to two boys on the spectrum, it became my mission to go above and beyond "acceptance" and what that might look like and mean to someone on the spectrum. So, I delved into the depths of Facebook where I became friends with those within the autism community. It was important to me that my boys had parents who were influenced by those who could relate and see life from their own eyes. This is how I met Luke. Luke is a beautiful soul who is inspirational, caring, thoughtful, compassionate and hardworking. Years of posts, stories, pictures and conversations that have shown me what brings happiness to Luke: talking about friends, family, hobbies, dreams, goals and memories. He's shown me the depths of his anxiety, depression, feelings of defeat, sadness ...like sharing memories of those he's lost despite how painful it is to revisit those losses. It's beautiful to see a person who loves and feels so deeply. Through it all, Luke pushes on, trying to shape a life where he'll be wholeheartedly accepted and understood, heard without having to speak, where the struggles are less, and the personal victories are more. Luke has shown me how I can be so much more for my boys. Despite all I've learned, I have a long way to go. Thank you for being you and for trusting me and accepting me to be a part of your life. Cheers to a long friendship!

CY

I know the lovely Luke from working with him at Wallace Fields Infant School. Luke is just the gentlest and kindest person who was amazing with the children. Despite feeling nervous, Luke always came into class with a smile and a willingness to turn his hand to anything. I miss working with you Luke, you would brighten up my days and always make the children smile. So proud of you making this book, you're amazing.

JS

I met Luke for the first time in late 2008 at Roehampton University where we were both studying, he in his first year and I in my last. We quickly discovered that we not only shared mutual friends but interests as well, chief among them football and Chelsea in particular.

That academic year of 2008-2009 will probably go down as the most fun in my entire life, and much of that was down to Luke.

We socialised and went to football together in what was the most carefree time that I can remember. I must say that, like most students, I also got up to no good sometimes, but none of this was down to Luke!

When that year ended, we went our separate ways but stayed in contact, occasionally meeting up to play golf and reminisce on our weird and wonderful university year. It also became clear to me that Luke was suffering from symptoms of depression and anxiety. I had no idea about this when we saw each other every day. Why would I, when he could only ever be seen laughing, smiling and joking without a care in the world? It was around this time that I myself finally began to seek help for similar problems and, while I am not out of the woods yet, I have begun to see the world in a different light and am finally able to empathise with Luke's issues fully and deeply. To be honest, I am a man of many passing acquaintances but very few true friendships, so it says something about the person Luke is that eleven years later I am prouder than ever to count him as a friend.

SC

I met Luke during my first year of 6th form through a mutual friend. I would be lying if I said we were great friends who were exceptionally close, however Luke very quickly became one of those friendships where you don't always need to see or even talk to then often but when you wanted to or more importantly, needed to, you knew he would be there. Ever willing to listen, offer advice and just be a friend, a real friend with complete honesty.

Over the years, work, kids and life overcame me and yet Luke still is that same friend, always checking in, always ready to listen and most importantly, always truly understanding. Luke, from way back then during 6th form as a teenager until now as an adult, has and is always putting others first, sometimes to his own detriment. Despite this, he remains true to his beliefs that there is goodness in all and sometimes all that's needed is someone to understand and always be there. Right there is what sums Luke up.

I'd like to take this opportunity to thank Luke for the years of undeserved checking in, years of undeserved understanding and years of undeserved friendship. Luke, more than 10 years on from our first meeting, remains one of the nicest people I've come to meet in my life, and I wish him nothing but happiness, love and success as it is all he deserves and has come a long way to accomplish.

EP

I met Luke at Roehampton University when we were both students there undertaking our respective degrees. The university was a very social place, including a section of the library called 'Wired'. As well as being a computer room for students to complete their work, it was also a place where people came together. It had a little cafe, circle-shaped tables and was open almost 24/7. I would write many of my essays there and is where I remember often talking with Luke. We also met at university events such as 'The Bop' on occasion and I remember always being happy to see him.

We have always got on very well and I find him a pleasure to be around. I find that I can have very good conversations with him because he is a great listener but also has great things to say in response.

Often, in my experience (due to being the talkative type) quiet people tend to just let me do the talking. With Luke, although he has a quiet demeanour, I find the conversational balance to be perfect.

He is kind, thoughtful and I feel this is why he sometimes finds social situations challenging. He puts so much thought into everything he says and does, and his brain never stops for rest. I can relate to this because sometimes I feel that my brain never stops, and I can become overwhelmed.

I have been on a similar journey to Luke and as such feel we are alike, which is why I think we have the strong friendship we have. I have recently been put on a waiting list to be diagnosed with ADHD and am suspected, at the age of 28, to be on the spectrum.

My favourite memory of us is when we met a few years after graduating due to me having to return to London for a training course.

We met in Waterloo (one of Luke's favourite places to go) and had a lovely catch up looking around Southbank and going to the Tate Gallery among other things. It was lovely to catch up with such a warm-hearted person and dear friend.

NR

Dearest Luke, apologies for not being in touch for such a long time, it has been one thing after another and then you realise how time flies by so quickly. I think what you're doing is incredible, and certainly brave to open yourself up the way that you are. I obviously met you at Wallace Fields Infant School and it was an absolute pleasure getting to work with you. You are kind and caring and that certainly showed, especially to the team and children. I know some days can be harder than others and how much of a challenge it is dealing with your emotions. I can only hope you find your way back to your old self with a little time and reflection because there are not enough kind and caring people in this world like yourself. I can truly say I'm honoured to have met such a lovely young man and I wish you, as always, the best in life.

HB

Luke is my cousin whom I have never met in person but is nonetheless an amazing relative and we have a close bond. I remember our first conversation involved us talking about travelling and how we could get a tent and live in Peru - I think that was what we discussed, or possibly it's just where I feel like going right now. We actually said we would work in a school there.

Ups and downs, we have experienced it all and talked it out with each other; forever unconditionally loving and supporting one another on this incredible roller coaster journey of life. I am so proud of all your achievements and how you never give up on what you believe in! No matter what life throws at him, Luke throws on his Superman cape and thrives in any challenge he faces. Being open about your feelings and expressing yourself authentically is beautiful and every person around you is blessed to be in your presence. Peace, love and light.

NM

I've known Luke for most of my life and one thing I've always noticed is his lovely smile. He has such a warm heart even from a young age. My family moved away from Roehampton when I reached adolescence and sadly, we lost touch.

We reconnected years later through social media and our bond was just as strong. He has had a rough time trying to figure himself out and fight for a diagnosis, but I don't think he realises how much he really does overcome his challenges.

Examples include when he pushed above and beyond by working abroad on two occasions, finishing his degree, and even finding his first relationship, all which were pivotal moments in his life so far.

I also suffer with mental health issues and find it hard to communicate but Luke is amazing at keeping in touch and expressing himself. Luke is a friend I know I will have for a lifetime and I can find comfort in that.

Don't change who you are Luke. Your struggles make you who you are, and you are probably one of the nicest people I know.

JE

Although I struggle to remember when we first met, I can only assume it was on the tennis courts at the Bank of England Sport Centre. What I do remember is you being the most incredibly kind and generous person who was always willing to help others, especially the kids in tennis sessions. A bit shy but always pushing himself to try get out there and do new things each day. I remember one time where I came to visit him in Epsom, and we spent a few hours at the local golf club. Was amazing to reconnect after a number of years and to see Luke hadn't changed. I hope you get the book published and it's a huge success brother.

SF

I first met Luke six years ago when I was going through a difficult time. I was struggling to manage my mental health and autism, respectively. Luke was like a light in the dark and as soon as I met him, he showed me warmth and acceptance. I will never forget that about Luke in how caring he is. We have met up in London and had a brilliant time catching up.

I am doing a lot better these days, but Luke will forever be in my heart. I consider it a beautiful honour to have a friend like him with so much compassion. I wish nothing but the best for him and know how much of a fighter he is; even when he is going through tough times himself, he always gives his time to others. Much love my dear friend.

JY

I met Luke approximately seven years ago on a Facebook group for people on the spectrum. I was around 22 at the time and was going through my own process of getting a diagnosis. Luke was one of the first people to contact me and ever since we have been close. He has helped guide, inspire and motivate me in my own struggles, despite him fighting his own respective battles.

Luke is one of the humblest people I've ever met and although we haven't had the pleasure of meeting in person, I consider him to be a wonderful friend of mine as we can talk about anything without fear or judgement. There is nothing but acceptance and support for one another. I hope this is the year that Luke can once and for all get the answers he has been seeking and finally better understand himself. With these diagnoses, through personal experience, it will help him be able to move forward in his life with the necessary support and guidance he deserves.

MH

We met while I was a camper at French Woods Festival. He was on the tennis staff and I remember how accepting he was, despite how much I struggled on the courts. I only played during the summer and I was a true beginner. Fast forward from 2008 to now and keeping in touch through all these years, we learned that we had a lot in common. This in turn really helped us understand each other, particularly with respect to our personal conditions. We both deal with a lot which I feel emphasises how we know how to support each other in such a caring way. Luke has always been there for me through thick and thin.

Personally, I suffer from multiple mental illnesses and similar to Luke, the doctors still haven't truly figured out what exactly I have. That being said, one thing that Luke and I have discussed many times, is how he only learned in his mid to late 20s that he had some form of mental health and/or ASD disorder. I ended up going into special education as a career and now work with children who suffer from numerous illnesses/disabilities which is something Luke never received in his school years. I applaud Luke for having the drive, despite all the struggles he faces with his anxiety and depression, to write this book. People who don't go through what we face each day don't understand the true struggles that come with mental health and ASD disorders.

Some final comforting words as I, Luke Miller-Ball, say thank you for reading my story so far. If I have even helped, given incentive, or given a better understanding to one person I will consider this venture a worthy one.

These two positive affirmations are quotes I have used a lot to help keep me going through some of the toughest times:

"I may not be where I want to be but thank God I'm not where I used to be. I am doing okay, and I am on my way."

"Treat people the way you want to be treated. Love people the way you want to be loved."

ALWAYS KEEP FIGHTING!

Printed in Great Britain
by Amazon

55645667R00179